Final Report for Emergency Stabilization and Rehabilitation Treatment Monitoring of the Keeney Pass, Cow Hollow, Double Mountain, and Farewell Bend Fires

By Troy A. Wirth and David A. Pyke

Open-File Report 2009-1152

U.S. Department of the Interior
U.S. Geological Survey

U.S. Department of the Interior
KEN SALAZAR, Secretary

U.S. Geological Survey
Suzette M. Kimball, Acting Director

U.S. Geological Survey, Reston, Virginia: 2009

For more information on the USGS—the Federal source for science about the Earth, its natural and living resources, natural hazards, and the environment, visit http://www.usgs.gov or call 1-888-ASK-USGS.

For an overview of USGS information products, including maps, imagery, and publications, visit *http://www.usgs.gov/pubprod*

To order this and other USGS information products, visit *http://store.usgs.gov*

Suggested citation:
Wirth, T.A., and Pyke, D.A., 2009, Final report for emergency stabilization and rehabilitation treatment monitoring of the Keeney Pass, Cow Hollow, Double Mountain, and Farewell Bend fires: U.S. Geological Survey Open-File Report 2009-1152, 62 p.

Contents

Contents—Continued

Figures

Figures—Continued

Tables

Conversion Factors

SI to Inch/Pound

Multiply	By	To obtain
centimeter (cm)	0.3937	inch (in.)
kilometer (km)	0.6214	mile (mi)
meter (m)	3.281	foot (ft)
hectare	2.471	acre
square meter (m^2)	0.0002471	acre

Final Report for Emergency Stabilization and Rehabilitation Treatment Monitoring of the Keeney Pass, Cow Hollow, Double Mountain, and Farewell Bend Fires

By Troy A. Wirth and David A. Pyke

Executive Summary

A strategy for monitoring post-fire seedings in the sagebrush steppe of the Intermountain West was developed and used to monitor four example fires in the Vale, Oregon District of the Bureau of Land Management (BLM). We began to develop a potential approach by (1) reviewing previous vegetation monitoring manuals produced by the Federal government to determine what techniques and approaches had been approved for use, and (2) monitoring a set of example fire rehabilitation projects from 2006 through 2008.

We reviewed seven vegetation monitoring manuals approved for use by the Federal government. From these seven manuals, we derived a set of design elements appropriate for monitoring post-fire rehabilitation and stabilization projects. These design elements consisted of objectives, stratification, control plots, random sampling, data quality, and statistical analysis. Additionally, we chose three quantitative vegetation field procedures that were objective and repeatable to be used in conjunction with these six design elements.

During the spring and summer of 2006 to 2008, U.S. Geological Survey personnel monitored vegetation in seven post-fire seeding treatments in four burned areas in the Vale district of the BLM in eastern Oregon. Treatments monitored included a native and non-native seeding in each of the Farewell Bend, Double Mountain, and Keeney Pass fires, and a native seeding at the Cow Hollow fire. All fires occurred in 2005.

There generally was a low level of plant establishment for all seedings by 2008. The quantitative objective established by the BLM was to achieve 5 seeded grass plants/m^2 by the end of 3 years as a result of the seeding. There was an estimated 3.97 and 6.28 plants/m^2 in 2006 and 1.06 and 0.85 plants/m^2 seeded perennial grasses in 2008 from the Keeney Pass non-native and native seeding, respectively. The Cow Hollow seeding resulted in the lowest establishment of perennial seeded grasses of the four project areas with 0.69 plants/m^2 in 2006 and 0.09 plants/m^2 in 2008. Density of seeded perennial grasses at the Double Mountain non-native and native seeding were 2.72 and 3.86 plants/m^2 in 2006 and 0.90 and 1.74 plants/m^2 in 2008, respectively. The Farewell Bend non-native seeding resulted in 5.62 plants/m^2 in 2006 and 0.42 plants/m^2 in 2008 while the native seeding had 2.22 seeded grass plants/m^2 in 2006 and 0.44 plants/m^2 by 2008. The primary reason for low level of establishment on most treatments except the Cow Hollow seeding was most likely the unfavorable timing and amount of precipitation in 2007 and 2008.

Measurements of density within the first 3 years provide the best estimate of initial seeding success. Increases in cover due to the seedings were not detectable in the first 3 years following seeding in this monitoring effort. Changes in cover resulting from the treatments may be detectable in cases where the seedings were very successful in the first 3 years following seeding, but in areas with lower annual average precipitation, may not occur consistently. As a result, cover of seeded species may not be a good indication of seeding success in the early years after treatment. However, cover is useful for monitoring initial patterns of abundance of naturally recovering vegetation, exotic annual grasses and forbs, and bare ground. Cover measurements at these four sites revealed patterns common to most of the treatment areas in cover of litter, bare ground, and exotic annuals in response to drill seeding and weather patterns. There was a rapid increase in litter at all treatments after the fire. Additionally, there was less litter in treatment plots than in the control plots in 2006 probably due to the mechanical action of the seed drill. There also was a corresponding decrease in bare ground from 2006 to 2008. Initially, higher bare ground cover at treatment plots appears to be due to the mechanical action of the seed drill.

Cover of annual grasses, primarily *Bromus tectorum*, increased from 2006 to 2007 and then decreased slightly in 2008. The highest cover and density of exotic annual grasses generally occurred in the second year following fire. Immediately after fire, lower densities of *B. tectorum* may emerge due to the loss of seed, but *B. tectorum* plants that do emerge often produce an abundance of seed due to high nutrient availability and reduced competition, resulting in higher densities the following year.

There was a consistent, negative linear relationship between the amount of cover of existing perennial grasses and annual grass cover at treatment areas. This relationship also was apparent in the gap data, and annual grass cover was greatest when basal gaps in the greater-than-200-cm size class were more frequent. The inverse relationship between cover of perennial and annual grasses suggests that post-fire seedings, when successful, can improve rangeland condition where annual invasive grasses are problematic.

Overall, quantitative objectives are a valuable part of monitoring the initial success of post-fire seedings. However, they need to be adapted for specific situations and areas. The potential of a particular area to reach a certain density or cover of desirable plant species (and the condition of the pre-fire plant community, for example, healthy or degraded) can be used to set initial objectives, which could be further modified by conditional statements that depend on environmental conditions after seeding. These conditional objectives may be developed to include a range of values rather than a specific target objective. Eventually, using data from many projects over time, a model could be developed to predict optimum seeding success over a range of conditions. Using such a dynamic approach to setting objectives would minimize the numbers of projects that are deemed failures due to unrealistic objectives or environmental factors that are outside the control of land management. Monitoring at the four areas from the Vale, Oregon District of the Bureau of Land Management that burned in 2005 also demonstrated potential uses and difficulties associated with monitoring ES&R (Emergency Stabilization and Rehabilitation) treatment effectiveness. Overall, the monitoring approach, combined with the quantitative techniques, performed reasonably well in burned areas previously dominated by sagebrush. Future monitoring efforts should take into account the logistical constraints of each design element and quantitative technique to arrive at the most cost-effective yet statistically valid monitoring plan. In the future, procedures that encompass more of the natural variability, either through sampling at more locations or incorporating the use of remote sensing may be able to capture more of the natural variability at the landscape scale.

The value of the three quantitative techniques for interpreting success of post-fire seedings depends on the time frame in which they will be used. For the first 3 years following seeding (the period for which monitoring is usually funded), density is the most directly applicable measurement of treatment effect and is emphasized in this report. Changes in plant cover and basal-gap intercept measurements are small during the first 3 years and, when combined with environmental and observer variation, could not be used for determining success. As the seeding ages and plants become larger, however, comparison of cover and gap-intercept data between treatment and control plots can be used to determine long-term effects. Whether initial densities in the first 3 years correlate to later cover and basal-gap intercept measurements is unknown and warrants further investigation.

In addition to assessing level of establishment at a variety of different post-fire seedings, the use of similar techniques to monitor Vale fires helped identify patterns common throughout multiple treatments. Consistent patterns of vegetation attributes identified in these four burned sites include the rate of accumulation of litter, the rate of decrease of bare ground, the inverse relationship between annual grass and forb cover, and the relationships between annual grasses with perennial grass cover and basal–gap intercept. Identifying additional patterns at a greater number of projects in a wider geographic area and correlating with site factors (such as soil, elevation, and climate) will aid efforts to improve seeding success through adaptive management.

Introduction

In 2004, the BLM requested that the U.S. Geological Survey (USGS) develop an approach to monitor the effectiveness of ES&R treatments in sagebrush ecosystems. We began to develop a potential approach by (1) reviewing previous vegetation monitoring manuals produced by the Federal government to determine what techniques and approaches had been approved for use, and (2) monitoring a set of example fire-rehabilitation projects from 2005 through 2008.

Review of Monitoring Manuals

We reviewed seven vegetation monitoring manuals approved for use by the Federal government. From these seven manuals, we derived a set of design elements appropriate for monitoring post-fire rehabilitation and stabilization projects. These design elements consisted of objectives, stratification, control plots, random sampling, data quality, and statistical analysis. Additionally, we chose three quantitative vegetation field methods that were objective and repeatable to be used in conjunction with these six design elements. We produced a report entitled "Monitoring post-fire vegetation projects: A common approach for non-forested ecosystems" (Wirth and Pyke, 2007) that described these elements and quantitative procedures.

Example Fires

During the spring and summer of 2005 through 2008, USGS personnel monitored seven burned areas in the Vale District of the BLM in eastern Oregon. The purposes of monitoring these fires were to test the methods outlined in Wirth and Pyke (2007) and determine how well they worked for evaluating seeding success.

These burned areas and year of burn were Cherry Creek (2003), Atkins Butte (2002), Trimbly (2002), Farewell Bend (2005), Double Mountain (2005), Keeney Pass (2005), and Cow Hollow (2005). Three burned areas sampled in 2005 (Cherry Creek, Atkins Butte, and Trimbly) were monitored only in the third year post-seeding to test and refine the techniques for subsequent monitoring projects. Because we did not monitor these fires in the first and second years, it was not possible to determine natural vegetation recovery from the seeding or to establish control plots. This report will focus on the Keeney Pass, Cow Hollow, Double Mountain, and Farewell Bend burned areas.

Methods

The six design elements identified in Wirth and Pyke (2007) were used to monitor fires from 2006 to 2008. These design elements are objectives, stratification, control plots, random sampling, data quality, and statistical analysis. We used the quantitative objectives developed by the BLM for the treatment areas at the four burned areas and were able to implement the other five design elements ourselves.

We monitored post-fire treatments using quantitative field methods described in Herrick and others (2005a, 2005b) in conjunction with the design elements described in Wirth and Pyke (2007). We randomly established permanent plots within each treatment area. Each plot consisted of three 50-m transects radiating from a central point spaced 120° apart. In some cases, there were multiple treatments associated with a fire. In these cases, each treatment was monitored separately (for example, native and non-native seedings). At each plot, line and surface photographs were taken, and information on plot location and soils was gathered. Along each transect, line-point intercept (cover), density, and basal gap measurements were taken. Data were entered into a Microsoft$^{©}$ Access database (Rangeland Health Database; http://usda-ars.nmsu.edu/monit_assess/rangedb_main.php) developed for these techniques. Data were either entered in the database in the field using tablet personal computers or later in the office after first being recorded on field datasheets.

Objectives

It is essential to define management and sampling objectives before implementation of any ES&R projects. As described in Elzinga and others (1998), management objectives are "clearly articulated descriptions of a measurable standard, desired state, threshold value, amount of change, or trend that you are striving to achieve for a particular plant population or habitat characteristics." Well-defined management objectives in a monitoring program perform two functions: first, they establish a standard to measure the degree of success; and second, they determine the appropriate indicators to measure. A standard protocol can then be followed for the measurement of each indicator; thus, data-collection activities are directly related to management objectives. Sampling objectives should be paired with each management objective and should specify the desired confidence level for the sampling effort. Quantitative objectives were written by the BLM for the Keeney Pass, Cow Hollow, Double Mountain, and Farewell Bend fires but did not include confidence levels.

Stratification

Stratification is the partitioning of treatment areas into monitoring units to reduce variation and increase precision of sampling efforts. Areas that may respond differently to ES&R treatments, such as different soil types or ecological sites, are good candidates for stratification. Rules for stratification of treatment areas into monitoring units should be created during the planning stage of an ES&R project. Stratification of the area for treatments and monitoring can be accomplished using a defined set of variables such as slope, aspect, elevation, treatment type, minimum size, soil type, or ecological site.

Stratification of the area within the fire perimeters consisted of separately monitoring drill seedings with different seed mixes and eliminating slopes greater than 20% where the seed drill was unlikely to cover. Therefore, data can only be extrapolated within each treatment area and for slopes less than 20%.

Control Plots

Control plots are locations within a proposed treatment area that are established prior to treatments and avoided when treatments are applied. Control plots provide a direct measurement of the treatment effect (for example, seeded plants) and also a measurement of natural recovery without treatment, helping to make a determination about whether or not treatments were necessary. In the absence of control plots, comparing measurements at treatment areas to established quantitative objectives can be used to determine treatment effectiveness.

Placement of control plots is an important pre-treatment activity. Control plots placed randomly within each monitoring unit will minimize the chances of bias and enable statistical inference. Control plots that are placed in adjacent untreated areas cannot be guaranteed to be similar to the treated areas, thereby reducing the value of the comparison. At the Keeney Pass, Cow Hollow, Double Mountain, and Farewell Bend burned areas, we marked areas for control plots before the seeding. Seeding operators avoided these areas, and control plots were subsequently established at these locations.

Random Sampling

Random sampling ensures that monitoring data are unbiased and representative of the monitoring units. Random sampling is essential for defensible determinations of treatment effectiveness. Monitoring data that are not collected using random sampling are subject to criticism that data only came from areas where treatments were effective, or that data were biased by the site-selection process. This raises doubts about conclusions drawn from such data. In addition, data that are not derived from random sampling cannot be extrapolated to the rest of the treatment area and are only valid at the plot where those data were collected. There are several different methods of random sampling that can be used to establish ES&R monitoring plots: simple random sampling, systematic random sampling, restricted random sampling, or two-stage sampling (Elzinga and others, 1998). It also is necessary to ensure that the sample is representative of the entire area that is being monitored. One of these methods of random sampling is essential to enable statistical inference over as much of treated area as possible.

At each treatment area, we generated a set of random points and used these for locations of treatment and control plots. We ensured that plots were scattered throughout the treatment area by either dividing treatment areas into equal areas and using one random plot in each area (restricted random sampling) or using random locations that were scattered throughout the treatment area (simple random sampling).

Data Quality

After collecting monitoring data, it is helpful to assess data quality. This can be done by examining measures of variability such as standard deviations, standard errors, and confidence intervals. Other parameters such as precision, minimum detectable change, and power also can be examined. The magnitude of these parameters can then be taken into consideration when making decisions about treatment success.

Confidence intervals can be easily constructed and displayed graphically to demonstrate the quality of the data for managers and researchers. For the fires discussed in this monitoring report, we constructed confidence intervals of the difference between the treatment and control for the parameters associated with the stated objectives as a measure of overall treatment success.

Statistical Analysis

Statistical analysis of monitoring data can consist of simple comparisons between treated and untreated areas, or between treated areas for two different time periods. Using graphical analysis to display these comparisons can provide more information to land managers than using t-tests or more complicated statistics (Di Stefano, 2004). We examined 80% confidence intervals of the difference between control and treatment populations for seeded species as a way to visualize the effect of seeding treatments and to show the data's variation. This technique uses the difference between the mean of the two populations of interest (treatment and control) and constructs a confidence interval around the difference in means. If the confidence interval does not include zero, then the treatment and control are considered statistically different from each other. In this report, eighty percent confidence intervals are used to be reasonably confident that a type I error (false-change error) will not be committed. This means we are 80% confident that we will detect a change when it does occur, but there is a 20% chance of concluding there was a change when there was not. This may seem like a low level of confidence, yet using an 80% confidence interval also helps to protect against type II errors. Type II errors, or missed-change errors, occur when a change actually occurred but was not detected. In management situations a missed-change error could be just as serious as a false-change error so it is important to protect against both types. There is an inverse relationship between type I and type II errors, meaning that very high percentage confidence intervals increase the risk of a type II error. For this reason, we have chosen to report 80% confidence intervals in this report.

Quantitative Field Methods

At each plot, a center point and the start and end of each transect were permanently marked with a metal or plastic stake. Two photographs were taken along each transect, one from the center of the plot looking down the transect and one surface photograph at a random location along each transect. Both information describing location (GPS coordinates, slope, aspect, topographic position) and soils (type, texture, depth) were collected. Additional information, such as presence of drill rows and offsite influences, was noted.

Three procedures for collecting vegetation information were used at each plot. These were line-point intercept, density (belt and quadrat), and basal-gap intercept (Herrick and others, 2005a). These three quantitative procedures measure indicators of three key attributes of rangeland health; soil and site stability, hydrologic function, and biotic integrity (Herrick and others, 2005a). Line-point intercept measures the aerial coverage and type of biota, the amount of soil protected from erosion by rock, litter, or biological crust cover, and the amount of bare soil exposed to potential wind or water erosion. Density measurements quantify the number of individuals of each plant species or functional group and when combined with cover data, provide a picture of the plant community at a site. Basal-gap intercept measurements quantify the size and amount of large gaps between plant bases, which can be used to track susceptibility to runoff and water erosion. Data for each parameter were first averaged over the three transects to derive a plot estimate. Plot estimates at all treatment and control plots were then averaged together to derive values for the entire monitoring unit.

Line-Point Intercept

At every meter along each 50-m transect, a pin was lowered to the ground at a 90° angle to the transect line. Each plant and type of soil surface that intercepted the pin was recorded at each point. Plants intercepted at each point were categorized as "top canopy," "lower canopy," or "basal cover." The soil surface was recorded as litter, bare soil, rock, moss, or the base of plant (Herrick and others, 2005a).

Several types of cover data were derived using the line-point intercept procedure and are presented in this report.

- *Vegetation-foliar cover* is the proportion of the soil surface covered by a vertical projection of a plant canopy (Herrick and others, 2005b) regardless of plant species or functional group. It is derived by counting only "top canopy" data from the line-point intercept technique. For example, if total foliar cover of perennial grasses was 20%, this would mean that 20% of the ground surface of an area had perennial grasses as the uppermost vegetation layer.
- *Basal cover* is the proportion of the soil surface covered by the base of perennial plants (for example, the stem of a perennial forb or the crown of a bunchgrass).
- *Bare-ground cover* is defined as surfaces that are not covered by aerial or basal vegetation, litter, rock, or biological soil crusts. Bare ground is a measure of the amount of area that is exposed to direct raindrop impact.
- *Species or functional-group* foliar cover is defined as the proportion of the total ground surface covered by a particular plant species or functional group. The foliar cover for each functional group is reported as though there were no other vegetation above it or below it so that cover of all species or functional groups may exceed 100%. For example, if there were 20% cover of deep-rooted perennial grasses and 20% cover of shallow-rooted perennial grasses, there could be a total of 40% of the ground surface covered by perennial grasses. But this is unlikely because some shallow-rooted perennial grasses occur underneath deep-rooted perennial grasses, resulting in vegetation foliar cover of less than 40%.

Density

Three different sizes of quadrats were used for density estimates. The largest was a belt transect. This belt typically was 6 × 50-m (300 m^2) and was used to determine the density of large and less-common plants. The intermediate size was a set of ten, 1 × 1-m quadrats that were placed at 5-m intervals along each 50-m transect with a randomly chosen beginning location between 0 and 4 m. This resulted in 30, 1 × 1-m quadrats per plot. Within these intermediate quadrats, we counted small, common target species including deep-rooted perennial grasses (seeded and unseeded) and seeded forbs and shrubs. If we did not encounter at least 10 individuals of any of the target species in the 1 × 1-m quadrats, we then searched for the plant using the belt transect. Within each 1 × 1-m quadrat, we placed a 20 × 20-cm subquadrat (0.04 m^2) that we used to estimate density of exotic annual grasses. Shallow-rooted perennial grasses such as *Poa secunda* (Sandberg's bluegrass) and *Poa bulbosa* (bulbous bluegrass) were not counted in any of the density quadrats due to the difficulty in identifying individuals. Cover data were used to measure the abundance of these two species.

We attempted to distinguish plants seeded in 2005 versus naturally occurring plants or plants seeded in prior (pre-2005) treatments. The original approach was to separate all plants into three size classes (A = seedling, B = juvenile, and C = adult). Theoretically, in the first year after a seeding, only size class A plants would be attributed to the seeding and in the second year, size classes A and B would be attributed to the seeding. This was supposed to allow the determination of the success of the seeding. In reality, some plants that were class B in the second year were potentially pre-existing plants. Likewise, some plants that were class C in the first or second year may have been highly vigorous seedlings. As a result, we modified our density procedure so that a determination about whether a plant was seeded or unseeded was made while reading plots, and each plant was explicitly labeled seeded or unseeded. This appears to be the most accurate method. As a result of this change in methods, 2007 data are not presented in this report. In 2008, plants were carefully separated into seeded and unseeded categories. In this report, density data from 2006 and 2008 are presented.

Basal-Gap Intercept

Along each 50-m transect, the starting and ending points of each gap between bases of perennial plants (grasses, shrubs, and forbs) were recorded. The total length of each gap was determined and placed into one of four gap-size classes (25–50, 51–100, 101–200, and 200+ cm). The percentage of the line occupied by each gap-size class was then determined.

Results and Discussion

The Keeney Pass, Cow Hollow, and Double Mountain burned areas had the same monitoring objectives. These were:

1. To establish seeded grass densities of 5 plants/m^2 by the end of the third growing season following the wildfire in the key area.

2. To limit *Bromus tectorum* (cheatgrass) density to not more than 100 plants/m^2 by the end of the third growing season following wildfire control.

3. To obtain a total percent cover (live plants, litter, standing dead, and gravel/rock) value of ± 10% of adjacent unburned rangeland on the same ecological site within two growing seasons following wildfire control.

4. To obtain seed production on 90% of the perennial native grass and forb plants and 70% of the bitterbrush plants that were burned relative to seed production on adjacent unburned rangeland on the same ecological site prior to reintroduction of livestock to the burned area.

Of these four quantitative objectives, monitoring by the USGS from 2006 to 2008 addressed objectives 1 and 2. Data were not collected on unburned, adjacent rangeland because it was not clear if the adjacent areas were equivalent to the burned area prior to the fire. Control plots were used to derive a direct measurement of treatment effect. The objective of the Farewell Bend seeding was to reach 5 seeded plants/m^2 by the end of the third year of monitoring.

Recent detailed soil surveys were not available for the Keeney Pass, Cow Hollow, and Double Mountain burned areas. Soils at the Farewell Bend burned area were within a recent soil survey; however, due to the small size of the treatment areas and the complexity of soils in the area, the soil surveys were not used to further stratify the treatment areas.

Weather

The 17-year average precipitation (1991–2007) for the area as measured using the Agrimet weather station, Ontario Oregon Weather Station (ONTO) in Ontario, Oregon, was 26.8 cm. This weather station is located at an elevation of 689 m (2,260 ft) and approximately 13 km northeast from Keeney Pass, 17 km northeast from Cow Hollow, 30 km northeast from Double Mountain, and 47 km southeast from Farewell Bend. The area received above average precipitation (36.6 cm) in 2006, and below average precipitation for water years 2007 (14.5 cm) and 2008 (16.0 cm) (Bureau of Reclamation, *http://www.usbr.gov/pn/agrimet/yearrpt.html*). Initial conditions for the seeding were excellent. Above average precipitation from October 2005 through January 2006 recharged soil moisture (fig. 1). February 2006 received approximately one-half of the average precipitation but this was ameliorated by above average rainfall in March and April 2006. After this, 23 of the following 26 months received below average precipitation with only 2 months of average rainfall and 1 month of above average rainfall. The early part of water year 2007 (September–December) almost reached average levels but was then followed by 6 months of less than average precipitation. Overall, 2006 was an excellent year for plant growth in terms of timing and amount of rainfall. Both timing and amounts of precipitation were extremely poor in 2007 and 2008, although 2008 was slightly better.

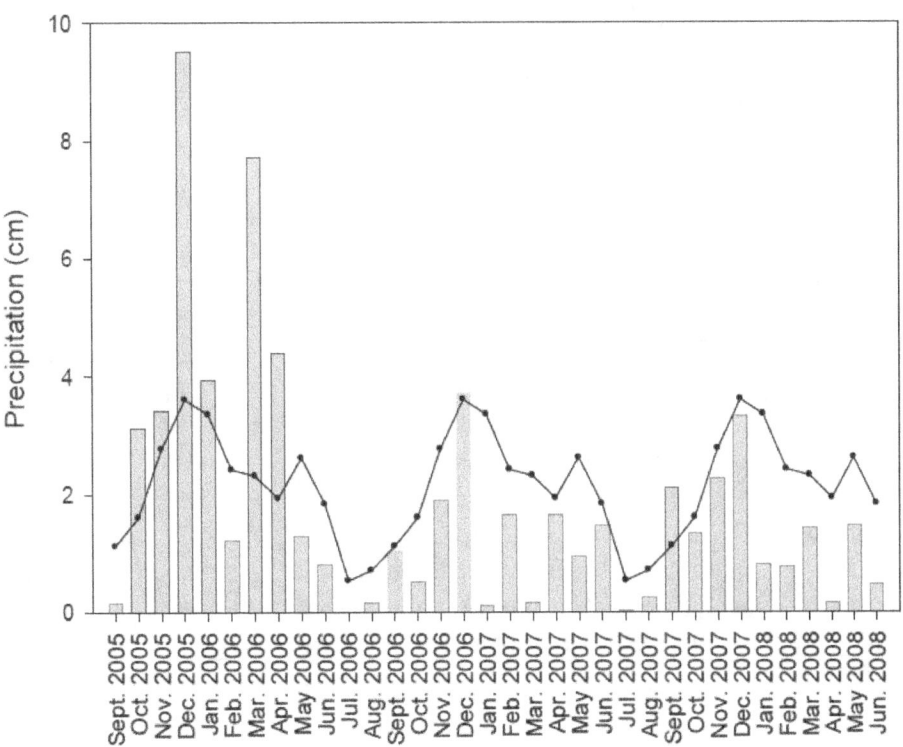

Figure 1. Precipitation received (bars) after treatment and average precipitation (line) at the Bureau of Reclamation Ontario weather station (ONTO) from September 2005 to June 2008. Blue outlined bars indicate above average precipitation for that month, red outlined bars indicate below average monthly precipitation, and gray bars indicate average monthly precipitation.

Keeney Pass

The Keeney Pass fire was sparked by lightning on August 8, 2005. It was ignited and contained on the same day, after burning a total of 1,481 ha (3,665 acres) of BLM land. The potential plant community in the burned area consists of an overstory of basin big sagebrush (*Artemisia tridentata* ssp. *tridentata*) and Wyoming big sagebrush (*Artemisia tridentata* ssp. *wyomingensis*) and an understory of deep rooted perennial grasses, such as *Achnatherum hymenoides* (Indian ricegrass), *Heterostipa comata* (needle and thread), *Pseudoroegneria spicata* (bluebunch wheatgrass) and *Achnatherum thurberianum* (Thurber's needlegrass), along with the shallow-rooted perennial grass *Poa secunda* (Sandberg bluegrass) (Bureau of Land Management, 2005a). The pre-fire plant community had changed significantly from this potential plant community and consisted of some perennial grasses, primarily *P. secunda* or previously seeded grasses *Agropyron cristatum* (crested wheatgrass) and *Elymus wawawaiensis* (Snake River wheatgrass) with *B. tectorum* and exotic annual forbs as common components. In some areas with deeper soils on the west side of Lincoln Bench, there are some remnant *Elymus cinereus* (basin wildrye) plants as well. Soils in the Keeney Pass area generally are silt loams similar to Nyssa silt loam. Nyssa silt loam is moderately deep and well-drained, mildly to moderately alkaline, and often with a weakly cemented pan. The elevations in the Keeney Pass area range from 795 to 885 m (2,608 to 2,903 ft).

Two drill seeding treatments were applied to the Keeney Pass fire burned area, a non-native seedmix of 210 ha (519 acres) and native seedmix of 865 ha (2,141 acres) (fig. 2). Correspondingly, we delineated two monitoring units. The native seeding monitoring unit consisted of areas of 0–20% slope that received drill seeding with the native seed mix (table 1). The non-native monitoring unit consisted of the areas of 0–20% slope that received drill seeding with the non-native seed mix. The seedmixes were not well documented and these species and rates are the best estimates for what was actually seeded. In the non-native treatment, seeded *P. spicata* was found at treatment plots even though it was not included in the documented seedmix.

Three of each control and treatment plots were placed within the non-native seeding, and five of each control and treatment plots were placed within the native seeding. One treatment plot, originally intended to be in the native seeding treatment, was inadvertently placed on private land and was subsequently removed. All plots were randomly placed within the respective treatment areas. The exact coordinates of the monitoring plots are given in appendix A, table A1 and soil information is presented in table A2

Within the perimeter of each treatment were previously seeded stands of perennial grasses, *A. cristatum* in the non-native seeding and *E. wawawaiensis* in the native seeding treatment. Due to the random location of plots, a different number of control and treatment plots were placed within these old seedings, causing a difference in initial values of vegetation parameters between control and treatment plots. In the non-native treatment, two treatment plots and one control plot were in the old *A. cristatum* seeding. In the native treatment, one treatment plot and two control plots were in the old *E. wawawaiensis* seeding.

Keeney Pass Non-Native Seeding

Densities of seeded grasses in the non-native seeding treatment plots were 3.97 plants/m^2 in 2006 and 1.06 plants/m^2 in 2008. Established seeded grasses were primarily *A. cristatum/A. fragile* (0.74 plants/m^2), *P. spicata* (0.18 plants/m^2), and *Thinopyron intermedium* (pubescent wheatgrass) (0.10 plants/m^2). From 2006 to 2008, seeded forbs decreased from 0.16 to 0 plants/m^2, and seeded shrubs were found at only 0.01 plants/m^2 by 2008 (table 2A). There were initial differences in densities of both non-seeded perennial grasses and *B. tectorum* between treatment and control plots resulting from differential plot placement within the old *A. cristatum* seedings. The density of non-seeded perennial grasses remained the same between 2006 and 2008 while the density of *B. tectorum* increased significantly in 2007 and decreased slightly in 2008.

Most gaps at both treatment and control plots in the non-native seeding were in the > 200 cm gap-size class (table 2B). During the 3-year monitoring period, there were no changes in percentages of transects occupied by any of the gap-size classes due to the seeding.

Vegetation foliar cover and bare ground decreased in treatment plots and remained constant in control plots from 2006 to 2008 (table 2C). Basal cover in treatment plots increased from 2.8 to 5.1% from 2006 to 2008, and increased less than 1% in control plots during the same time period. Functional group foliar cover of deep-rooted perennial grasses were initially different due to the unequal distribution of plots in the old *A. cristatum* seeding. Foliar cover of both deep- and shallow-rooted grasses were within 2% in all 3 years of monitoring in treatment plots (table 2D). Shallow-rooted perennial grasses in control plots showed higher variability and decreased from 13.8% in 2006 to 9.3% in 2007, and then increased to 17.1% in 2008. There were no detectable differences in cover of deep- or shallow-rooted perennial grasses, forbs, or shrubs due to the seeding. Foliar cover of exotic grasses, primarily *B. tectorum,* increased in 2007 and decreased in 2008, and cover of exotic annual forbs followed the opposite pattern, with a substantial decrease in 2007 followed by an increase in 2008. Cover of litter increased 47% in treatment and 20% in control plots over the 2006 to 2008 monitoring period.

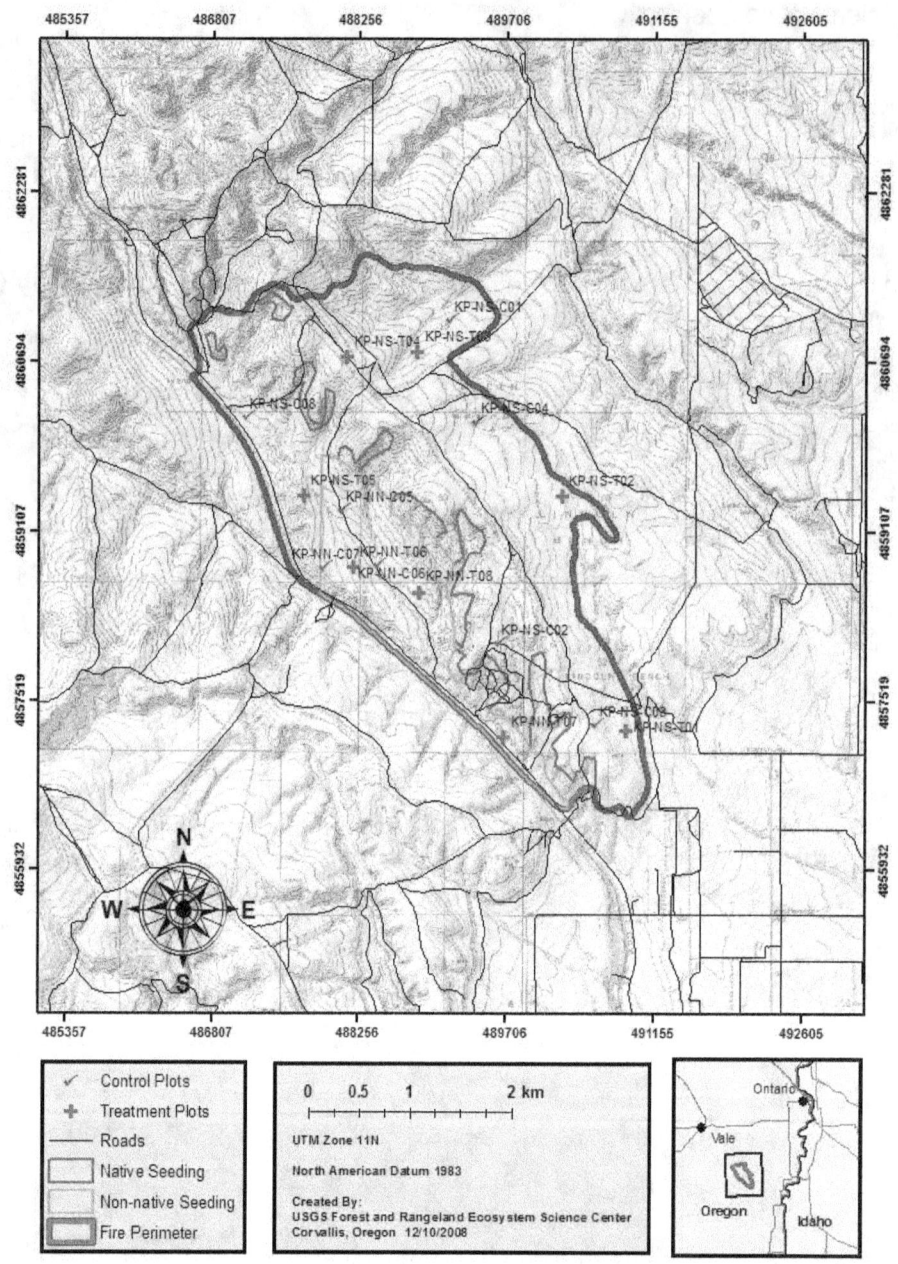

Figure 2. Location of burned and treated area, monitoring units, and monitoring plots within the Keeney Pass Fire (2005).

Table 1. Seed mixes used in native and non-native drill seedings at the 2005 Keeney Pass burned area, Oregon.

Native seed mix[a]	PLS[b] (lb/acre)	Non-native seed mix[a]	PLS[b] (lb/acre)
'Anetone' bluebunch wheatgrass (*Pseudoroegneria spicata*)	6.00	'Vavilov' Siberian wheatgrass (*Agropyron fragile*)	0.57
'Trailhead' basin wildrye (*Elymus cinereus*)	1.00	'P27' Siberian wheatgrass (*Agropyron fragile*)	2.27
'Luna' pubescent wheatgrass (*Thinopyron intermedium*)	0.34	'Fairway' crested wheatgrass (*Agropyron cristatum*)	1.14
'Arriba' western wheatgrass (*Pascopyrum smithii*)	0.17	'Hycrest' wheatgrass (*Agropyron cristatum*)	1.70
'Ladak' alfalfa (*Medicago sativa*)	0.40	'Nordan' crested wheatgrass (*Agropyron cristatum*)	0.40
'Apar' Lewis flax (*Linum lewisii*)	0.10	'Trailhead' basin wildrye (*Elymus cinereus*)	1.02
'Eski' sainfoin (*Onobrychis viciifolia*)	0.40	'Luna' pubescent wheatgrass (*Thinopyron intermedium*)	1.02
Fourwing saltbush (*Atriplex canescens*)	0.03	'Ladak' alfalfa (*Medicago sativa*)	0.23
Wyoming big sagebrush (*Artemisia tridentata* ssp. *wyomingensis*)	0.01	'Eski' sainfoin (*Onobrychis viciifolia*)	0.40
		'Apar' Lewis flax (*Linum lewisii*)	0.11
		Fourwing saltbush (*Atriplex canescens*)	0.06
		Wyoming big sagebrush (*Artemisia tridentata* ssp. *wyomingensis*)	0.01
TOTAL	8.45	TOTAL	8.93

[a]Seedmixes are named native or non-native depending on the species that compose the majority of the seedmix. Single quotes surround registered cultivar names for species.

[b]PLS = pure live seed

Keeney Pass Non-Native Seeding Conclusions

The density objectives for seeded perennial grasses and exotic grasses (*B. tectorum*) were not met at the Keeney Pass non-native seeding. Established seeded-grass density was estimated to be between 0.47 and 1.65 plants/m^2 with a mean of 1.06 plants/m^2 (80% confidence, fig. 3). An estimated 10,600 perennial grass plants/ha were established as a result of the seeding, and this is a significant increase compared to the control plots (fig. 3). There were no significant differences between the treatment and control for seeded shrub (*A. tridentata*) and forb species (fig. 3). Density of *B. tectorum* was 6 to 12 times higher than the 100 plants/m^2 target objective in all years of monitoring (table 2A). Disturbances of fire and drill seeding combined with climate and competition from naturally recovering vegetation seemed to play a greater role in population dynamics of *B. tectorum* than the newly established seeded plants. The relatively low density and small size of seeded plants had little effect on the density of *B. tectorum* at this early stage in the seeding.

Table 2. Density of plants by functional group and *Bromus tectorum* (A), average percentage of each transect composed of basal gaps within each gap-size class (B), vegetation foliar cover, bare ground, and basal cover (C), and functional group foliar cover (D) at the Keeney Pass non-native seeding, Oregon, 2006–08.

A.

Functional group[a]	Non-native seeding treatment (plants/m^2)[b]		Non-native seeding control (plants/m^2)[b]	
	2006	2008	2006	2008
NS perennial grass	1.73 (0.82)	1.81 (0.93)	0.40 (0.40)	0.412 (0.42)
NS shrubs	0.14 (0.11)	0.00	0.09 (0.08)	0.01 (0.01)
SD perennial grass	3.97 (1.01)	1.06 (0.31)	0.01 (0.01)	0.00
SD shrubs	0.00	0.01 (0.01)	0.00	0.00
SD forbs	0.16 (0.06)	0.00	0.02 (0.02)	0.00

	2006	2007	2008	2006	2007	2008
B. tectorum	633 (176)	1220 (383)	1091 (362)	949 (205)	1474 (376)	1190 (422)

[a]NS, non-seeded; SD, seeded. Density of NS perennial grasses does not include the shallow-rooted species, *Poa secunda* or *Poa bulbosa*.

[b]Numbers in parentheses are standard errors.

B.

Gap size (cm)	Non-native seeding treatment (percent of line)			Non-native seeding control (percent of line)		
	2006	2007	2008	2006	2007	2008
25–50	6.4	7.9	7.7	5.0	5.2	5.1
51–100	11.4	8.4	11.7	7.0	6.5	6.6
101–200	14.6	12.3	13.3	5.9	5.2	4.6
>200	57.4	61.5	56.9	74.7	75.3	74.4

C.

Cover	Non-native seeding treatment (percent cover)			Non-native seeding control (percent cover)		
	2006	2007	2008	2006	2007	2008
Vegetation foliar cover	79.3	75.7	67.6	81.5	79.1	79.6
Bare ground	18.1	17.0	12.7	7.3	7.0	6.4
Basal cover	2.8	3.1	5.1	1.5	2.2	2.4

Table 2. Density of plants by functional group and *Bromus tectorum* (A), average percentage of each transect composed of basal gaps within each gap-size class (B), vegetation foliar cover, bare ground, and basal cover (C), and functional group foliar cover (D) at the Keeney Pass non-native seeding, Oregon, 2006–08.—Continued

D.

Functional Group Foliar Cover[a]	Non-native seeding treatment (percent cover)[b]			Non-native seeding control (percent cover)[b]		
	2006	2007	2008	2006	2007	2008
DR perennial grass	13.6 (7.2)	13.1 (7.7)	15.6 (8.5)	4.9 (4.9)	4.4 (4.4)	5.8 (5.8)
SR perennial grass	13.3 (12.7)	11.8 (11.1)	13.3 (12.7)	13.8 (13.8)	9.3 (9.3)	17.1 (16.8)
Perennial forbs	0.4 (0.4)	0.2 (0.2)	0.4 (0.2)	0.2 (0.2)	3.3 (2.4)	0.9 (0.6)
Shrubs	0.0 (0.0)	0.0 (0.0)	0.0 (0.0)	0.2 (0.2)	0.2 (0.2)	0.0 (0.0)
Exotic annual grass	52.0 (12.0)	56.2 (14.8)	40.4 (16.8)	66.9 (11.1)	70.7 (15.5)	59.3 (19.7)
Exotic annual forbs	14.9 (5.7)	1.1 (0.8)	7.8 (3.5)	10.9 (3.1)	3.8 (2.6)	8.4 (3.9)
Litter	20.7 (5.0)	51.3 (2.0)	67.8 (6.0)	65.1 (14.6)	79.6 (13.5)	85.3 (6.3)

[a]DR, deep-rooted; SR, shallow-rooted; Exotic annual grasses primarily *B. tectorum*.

[b]Numbers in parentheses are standard errors.

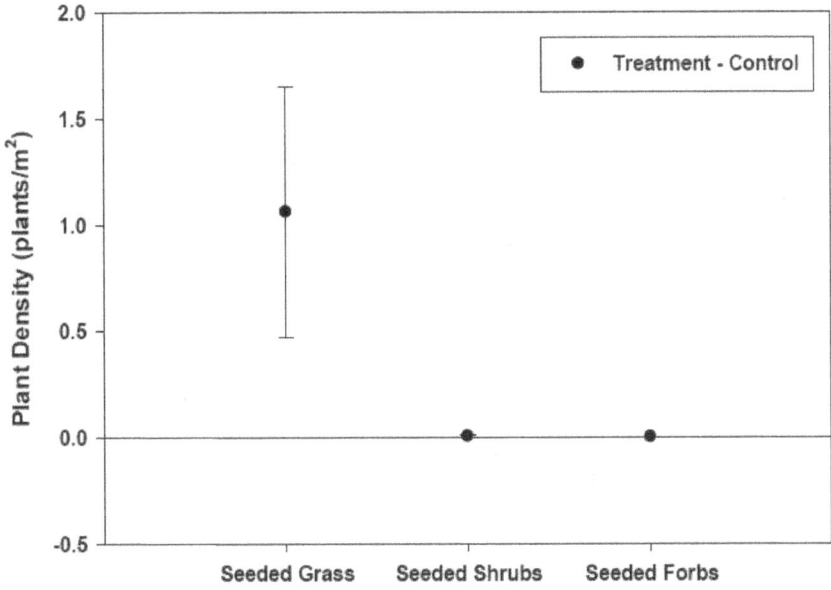

Figure 3. Confidence interval (80%) of the difference between treatment and control densities of seeded grasses, shrubs, and forbs at the Keeney Pass non-native seeding, Oregon, 2008.

Keeney Pass Native Seeding

Densities of seeded grasses at the native-seeding treatment plots decreased from 6.28 plants/m^2 in 2006 to 0.85 plants/m^2 in 2008 (table 3A). Established seeded grasses in 2008 primarily were *P. spicata* (0.35 plants/m^2), *T. intermedium* (0.15 plants/m^2), and unknown, non-reproducing grasses (0.33 plants/m^2). Of the four treatment plots, one had few seeded plants in 2006 and none in 2008. The other three plots had substantially more seeded grasses with a range of 4.10 to 14.00 plants/m^2 in 2006, which decreased to 0.20 to 1.60 plants/m^2 in 2008. Seeded sagebrush decreased from 0.93 to 0.11 plants/m^2 and seeded forbs decreased from 1.25 to 0.08 plants/m^2 during the same time period.

There also was a large increase in the density of *B. tectorum* (451 to 1,309 plants/m^2) in treatment plots from 2006 to 2007 but less of an increase at control plots (450 to 764 plants/m^2) during the same time. In general, establishment was very patchy and areas with high seedling establishment tended to be on locations that were previously occupied by sagebrush that had been burned to mineral soil with no remaining litter (fig. 4).

Most gaps in control plots and treatment areas were > 200 cm (table 3B). There were no significant (greater than 5%) changes in the percentages of gaps of each of the four classes over the 3-year monitoring period at either treatment areas or control plots. There also were no differences between control plots and treatment areas in any of the gap-size classes except for a slight initial difference between the 101–200 cm gap-size class, with treatment plots having a slightly greater percentage of gaps in this size class than the control plots (18.9 versus 11.1% in the treatment and control plots in 2006, respectively).

Overall vegetation foliar cover at treatment and control plots increased slightly from 2006 to 2008 (table 3C). There was initially a higher percentage of bare ground at treatment plots in 2006 (26.1 versus 16.6%). By 2008, enough litter and cover had accumulated that treatment and control plots had similar amounts of exposed soil.

Overall, deep-rooted perennial grasses increased slightly from 2006 to 2008 in both treatment and control plots (table 3D). Shallow-rooted perennial grasses increased in treatment plots from 2006 to 2008 and stayed stable at control plots in 2006 and 2008, with a decrease in 2007. Cover of exotic forbs, primarily *Erodium cicutarium* (redstem storksbill) and *Salsola tragus* (salsify), generally followed the pattern of precipitation with higher cover in 2006, lower cover in 2007, and slightly higher cover in 2008. Cover of *B. tectorum* increased from 2006 to 2007 and decreased in 2008. Cover of litter was initially different between treatment and control plots in 2006 but had reached equivalent values by 2008 (77.7 versus 72.0%).

Table 3. Density of plants by functional group and *Bromus tectorum* (A), average percentage of each transect composed of basal gaps within each gap-size class (B), vegetation foliar cover, bare ground, and basal cover (C), and functional group foliar cover (D) at the Keeney Pass native seeding, Oregon, 2006–08.

A.

Functional group[a]	Native seeding treatment (plants/m²)[b]		Native seeding control (plants/m²)[b]	
	2006	2008	2006	2008
NS perennial grass	0.62 (0.34)	0.63 (0.33)	2.04 (0.95)	2.08 (0.98)
NS shrubs	0.00	0.00	0.00	0.00
SD perennial grass	6.28 (2.93)	0.85 (0.43)	0.13 (0.10)	0.00
SD shrubs	0.93 (0.52)	0.11 (0.08)	0.00	0.00
SD forbs	1.25 (0.57)	0.08 (0.07)	0.03 (0.02)	0.00

	2006	2007	2008	2006	2007	2008
B. tectorum	451 (166)	1,309 (225)	918 (178)	450 (214)	764 (336)	751 (341)

[a]NS, non-seeded; SD, seeded. Density of NS perennial grasses does not include the shallow-rooted species, *Poa secunda* or *Poa bulbosa*.

[b]Numbers in parentheses are standard errors.

B.

Gap size (cm)	Native seeding treatment (percent of line)			Native seeding control (percent of line)		
	2006	2007	2008	2006	2007	2008
25–50	7.3	7.5	7.4	9.3	9.6	11.1
51–100	11.6	11.9	10.4	11.1	11.8	11.5
101–200	18.9	16.9	18.0	11.1	10.1	9.1
>200	51.6	53.2	53.2	53.1	52.0	48.5

C.

Cover	Native seeding treatment (percent cover)			Native seeding control (percent cover)		
	2006	2007	2008	2006	2007	2008
Vegetation foliar cover	70.0	74.8	75.7	75.4	76.4	78.9
Bare ground	26.1	20.2	8.0	16.6	12.9	8.8
Basal cover	2.7	4.2	3.3	3.2	5.2	7.3

Table 3. Density of plants by functional group and *Bromus tectorum* (A), average percentage of each transect composed of basal gaps within each gap-size class (B), vegetation foliar cover, bare ground, and basal cover (C), and functional group foliar cover (D) at the Keeney Pass native seeding, Oregon, 2006–08.—Continued

D.

Functional Group Foliar Cover[a]	Native seeding treatment (percent cover)[b]			Native seeding control (percent cover)[b]		
	2006	2007	2008	2006	2007	2008
DR perennial grass	7.0 (3.2)	6.7 (2.8)	7.5 (4.4)	19.7 (10.5)	19.3 (3.5)	22.4 (12.1)
SR perennial grass	14.5 (5.1)	19.0 (6.0)	19.2 (5.7)	23.6 (10.4)	18.5 (7.4)	24.9 (10.1)
Perennial forbs	0.7 (0.5)	0.3 (0.2)	0.5 (0.3)	0.7 (0.5)	1.6 (1.1)	0.5 (0.3)
Shrubs	0.0	0.0	0.2 (0.2)	0.0	0.0	0.0
Exotic annual grass	51.0 (8.7)	64.7 (8.8)	57.3 (8.3)	38.8 (14.7)	46.1 (18.0)	29.1 (15.8)
Exotic annual forbs	12.0 (6.2)	5.5 (1.3)	7.5 (2.7)	16.9 (8.2)	7.7 (4.8)	9.1 (5.6)
Litter	25.2 (14.2)	51.7 (10.3)	77.7 (5.3)	47.1 (15.2)	65.7 (11.8)	72.0 (10.8)

[a]DR, deep-rooted; SR, shallow-rooted; Exotic annual grasses primarily *B. tectorum*.

[b]Numbers in parentheses are standard errors.

Keeney Pass Native Seeding Conclusions

The density of seeded species in 2008 did not reach the original objective of 5 plants/m^2 at the Keeney Pass native seeding. Density of seeded grasses were estimated to be between 0.14 and 1.56 plants/m^2 with a mean of 0.85 plants/m^2 (80% confidence, fig. 5). An estimated 8,500 plants/ha were established as a result of the seeding, and this is a significant increase compared to the control (fig. 5). There were no significant differences between treatment and controls for seeded forbs and shrubs, although some plants did establish in the treatment area (fig. 5). Density of *B. tectorum* was significantly higher than the 100 plants/m^2 objective (table 3A), and, as previously noted, demographics of *B. tectorum* seemed to be primarily driven by recent disturbance and climatic conditions rather than competition with seeded plants in the initial 3 years at the Keeney Pass non-native seeding.

Cow Hollow

The Cow Hollow fire occurred at the same time as the Keeney Pass fire (ignited and contained on August 8, 2005) and burned a total of 315 ha (779 acres) (Bureau of Land Management, 2005a, fig. 6). The potential plant community is similar to that described for the Keeney Pass area due to the close proximity of the two burned areas. The potential plant community in the area is a shrub overstory of primarily Wyoming big sagebrush (*A. tridentata* ssp. *wyomingensis*) with deep-rooted perennial grasses such as *A. hymenoides* (Indian ricegrass), *H. comata* (needle and thread) and *P. spicata* (bluebunch wheatgrass) and *A. thurberianum* (Thurber's needlegrass) along with the shallow-rooted perennial grass *P. secunda* (Sandberg bluegrass). In many areas within the burn perimeter, *P. secunda* forms dense patches with very few of the deeper rooted perennial grasses present. Additionally, some areas within the seeding have been previously seeded with *A. cristatum*.

Figure 4. Increased establishment and growth of seeded plants under burned sagebrush canopies, Keeney Pass burned area, Oregon. Photograph taken by Troy Wirth, May 18, 2007.

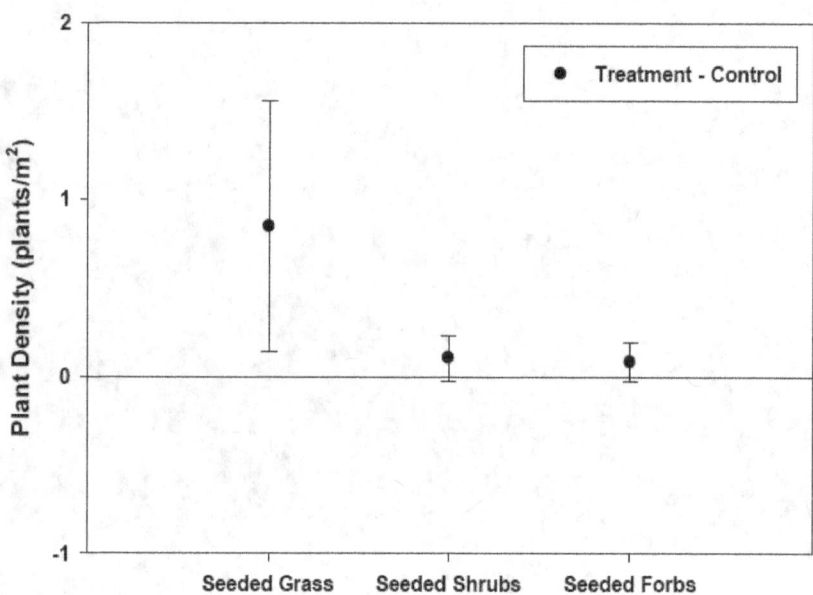

Figure 5. Confidence interval (80%) of the difference between treatment and control densities of seeded grasses, shrubs, and forbs at the Keeney Pass native seeding, Oregon, 2008.

Soils at the Cow Hollow treatment area were Nyssa silt loams. Nyssa silt loam is moderately deep and well-drained, and mildly to moderately alkaline. It often has a weakly cemented pan (Oregon State Water Resources Board, 1969). The elevation at the Cow Hollow burned area ranged from 815 to 845 m (2,673 to 2,772 ft).

The native seedmix applied at the Keeney Pass fire was also applied to the Cow Hollow burned area. The entire 315 ha were treated. The monitoring unit consisted of all areas that were drilled with the native seed mix between 0 and 20% slopes. Within this monitoring unit, we randomly placed five treatment and four control plots.

Seeded grass densities at the treatment plots were 0.69 plants/m^2 in 2006 and 0.09 plants/m^2 in 2008 (table 4A). Seeded grasses were primarily *T. intermedium* (0.04 plants/m^2), and *P. spicata* (0.04 plants/m^2). Seeded forb densities were 0.14 plants/m^2 in 2006 and 0.04 plants/m^2 in 2008. Density of sagebrush seedlings were 0.05 plants/m^2 in 2006 and 0.01 plants/m^2 in 2008. Density of *B. tectorum* increased significantly in 2007 and increased again slightly in 2008.

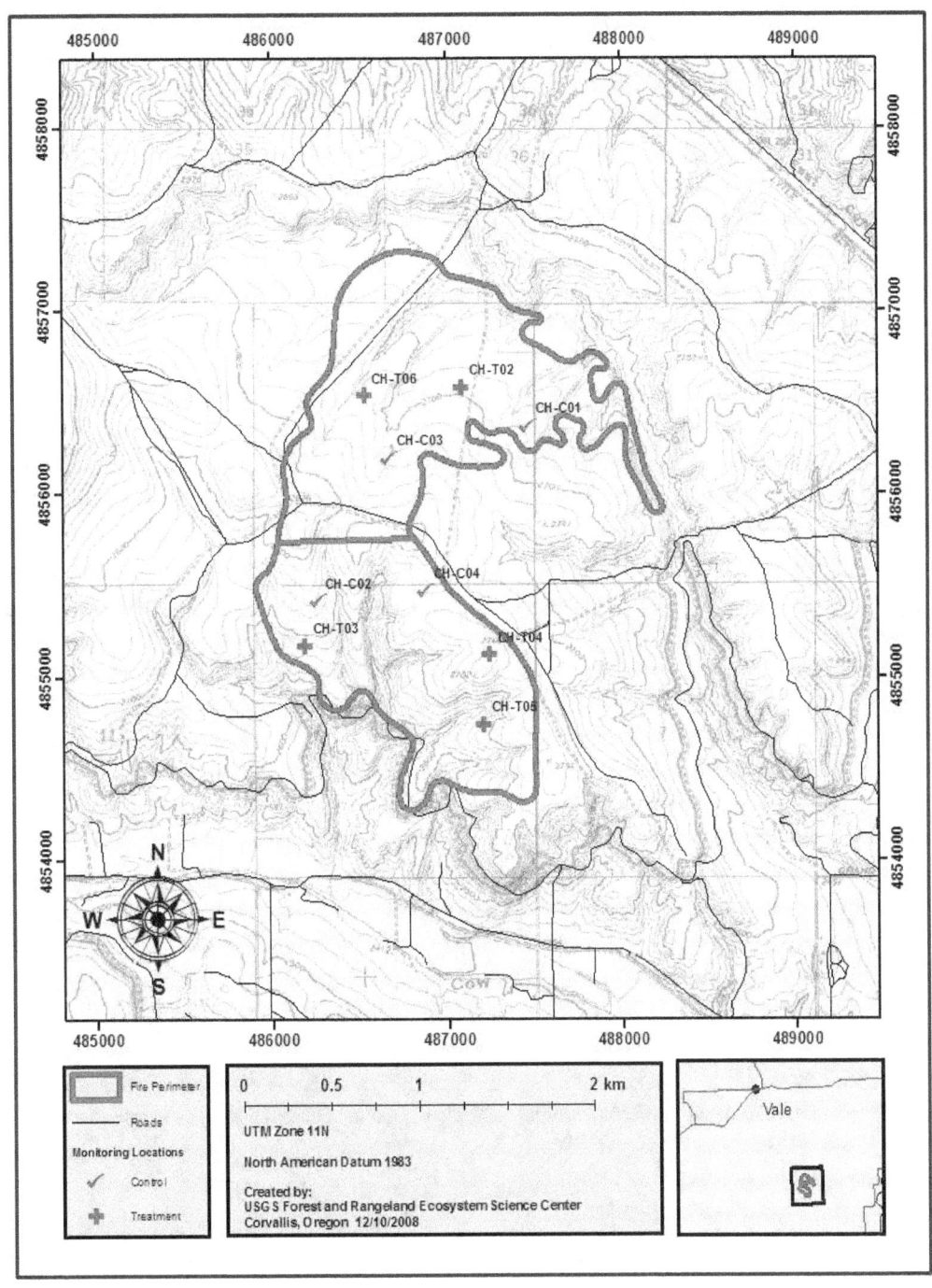

Figure 6. Location of Cow hollow fire burned and treated area including treatment and control plots, Oregon, 2006–08.

Basal gaps were highest in the > 200 cm size class from 2006 to 2008 (table 4B). However, while > 200 cm basal gaps were most prevalent, the percentage in this size class was lower than other treatment areas (for example, Keeney Pass) due to a large abundance of *P. secunda*. The *P. secunda* often existed in a wide range of sizes, from large, well-defined bunches to small, amorphous bunches interspersed with dead areas and single tillers (fig. 7). In this situation, very small plants are difficult to see, which increased variability between observers and years. Although variable, the data show a decrease in gaps in the > 200 cm size class from 2006 to 2008.

Vegetation foliar cover increased slightly in both treatment and control plots in 2007 and then decreased slightly from 2007 to 2008 (table 4C). There was a similar amount of bare ground at both treatment and control plots in 2006 (23.3 versus 23.5%) which subsequently decreased to 7.3 and 8.7% in the treatment and control plots by 2008.

Functional group foliar cover of deep-rooted perennial grasses at the Cow Hollow seeding was low and stayed low throughout the monitoring period (table 4D). In contrast, shallow-rooted perennial grasses (*P. secunda*) were abundant but changed little. Cover of exotic annual grasses increased in 2007 and decreased in 2008. Cover of exotic annual forbs declined in both 2007 and 2008. Cover of litter increased significantly from 2006 to 2008 at the treatment and control plots.

Table 4. Density of plants by functional group and *Bromus tectorum* (A), average percentage of each transect composed of basal gaps within each gap-size class (B), vegetation foliar cover, bare ground, and basal cover (C), and functional group foliar cover (D) at the Cow Hollow native seeding, Oregon, 2006–08.

A.

Functional group[a]	Native seeding treatment (plants/m²)[b]		Native seeding control (plants/m²)[b]	
	2006	2008	2006	2008
NS perennial grass	1.79 (1.21)	1.27 (0.97)	1.48 (0.68)	1.35 (0.71)
NS shrubs	0.04 (0.03)	0.04 (0.02)	0.01 (0.01)	0.01 (0.01)
SD perennial grass	0.69 (0.23)	0.09 (0.04)	0.03 (0.03)	0.00
SD shrubs	0.05 (0.05)	0.01 (0.00)	0.00	0.00
SD forbs	0.14 (0.05)	0.04 (0.03)	0.00	0.00

	2006	2007	2008	2006	2007	2008
B. tectorum	544 (263)	1133 (320)	1220 (319)	654 (276)	1240 (344)	1394 (373)

[a]NS, non-seeded; SD, seeded. Density of NS perennial grasses does not include the shallow-rooted species, *Poa secunda* or *Poa bulbosa*.

[b]Numbers in parentheses are standard errors.

B.

Gap size (cm)	Native seeding treatment (percent of line)			Native seeding control (percent of line)		
	2006	2007	2008	2006	2007	2008
25–50	13.7	16.2	17.2	1.0	11.6	10.3
51–100	14.7	15.2	14.8	12.6	14.4	18.6
101–200	15.3	14.8	13.5	20.2	20.3	19.2
>200	35.4	30.5	28.9	43.6	35.2	34.7

Table 4. Density of plants by functional group and *Bromus tectorum* (A), average percentage of each transect composed of basal gaps within each gap-size class (B), vegetation foliar cover, bare ground, and basal cover (C), and functional group foliar cover (D) at the Cow Hollow native seeding, Oregon, 2006–08.—Continued

C.

Cover	Native seeding treatment (percent cover)			Native seeding control (percent cover)		
	2006	2007	2008	2006	2007	2008
Vegetation foliar cover	71.3	77.1	76.3	73.3	77.3	73.0
Bare ground	23.3	11.1	7.3	23.5	12.7	8.7
Basal cover	4.7	6.0	6.8	4.3	6.7	5.2

D.

Functional Group Foliar Cover[a]	Cow Hollow treatment (percent cover)[b]			Cow Hollow control (percent cover)[b]		
	2006	2007	2008	2006	2007	2008
DR perennial grass	2.9 (2.3)	3.2 (2.7)	4.4 (3.3)	5.3 (3.0)	4.7 (2.4)	5.5 (3.6)
SR perennial grass	28.3 (5.4)	26.5 (5.0)	30.4 (5.0)	24.2 (2.9)	23.0 (5.4)	22.7 (5.3)
Perennial forbs	0.40 (0.3)	2.0 (1.0)	2.3 (1.1)	0.8 (0.3)	1.2 (1.0)	1.0 (0.6)
Shrubs	0.3 (0.2)	0.3 (0.2)	0.5 (0.4)	0.0 (0.0)	0.0 (0.0)	0.3 (0.3)
Exotic annual grass	50.1 (10.4)	59.3 (11.9)	53.6 (12.9)	54.0 (10.6)	61.3 (13.1)	52.8 (12.4)
Exotic annual forbs	5.2 (2.4)	2.8 (1.3)	1.6 (0.7)	7.3 (7.1)	2.7 (1.4)	2.3 (1.1)
Litter	24.8 (5.5)	57.20 (2.9)	76.1 (6.5)	19.8 (9.1)	61.5 (9.3)	78.2 (6.0)

[a]DR, deep-rooted; SR, shallow-rooted; Exotic annual grasses primarily *B. tectorum*.

[b]Numbers in parentheses are standard errors.

Cow Hollow Conclusions

Seeded grass densities at the Cow Hollow native seeding were estimated to be between 0.04 and 0.15 plants/m^2 with a mean of 0.09 plants/m^2. Despite this low level of establishment, seeded grass establishment was significantly higher than control plots (fig. 8). There were no differences between treatment and control for densities of seeded forbs or shrubs, although some forbs did establish in the treatment area. *B. tectorum* densities were also much higher than the 100 plants/m^2 target objective (table 4A).

Within the Cow Hollow burned area, there were many areas of dense, pre-fire *P. secunda* plants. In most of the treatment area, it was difficult to discern drill rows due either to frozen soil at the time of drilling or failure of the drill to cut through the dense mat of *P. secunda*. This may have resulted in much of the seed being placed directly on the soil surface where the chance of establishment was reduced. Additionally, the dense mat of amorphous bunches of *P. secunda* significantly increased the variability of the basal-gap intercept data. This effect was compounded by variable amounts and timing of precipitation. In this situation, meaningful conclusions regarding the short-term basal-gap intercept measurements are difficult to make at the Cow Hollow native seeding.

In other drill seedings, an increase in bare ground in the treatment plots compared to control plots was observed. This did not occur at the Cow Hollow seeding (table 4C), which may indicate that the seed drill was unable to properly bury the seed due to dense *P. secunda* or other site conditions and thus led to low seeded plant densities.

There were no detectable differences in cover of perennial grasses due to the seeding after 3 years. Although there were very high levels of perennial grass cover at the Cow Hollow seeding, most of the cover was due to the shallow-rooted *P. secunda*. This level of cover certainly provides protection from soil erosion, yet it may not help to meet other goals of land management, such as suitable wildlife habitat.

Figure 7. Abundant and small *secu* plants that resulted in unusual basal gap variability were found at the Cow Hollow burned area, Oregon. Photograph by USGS staff, May 12, 2007.

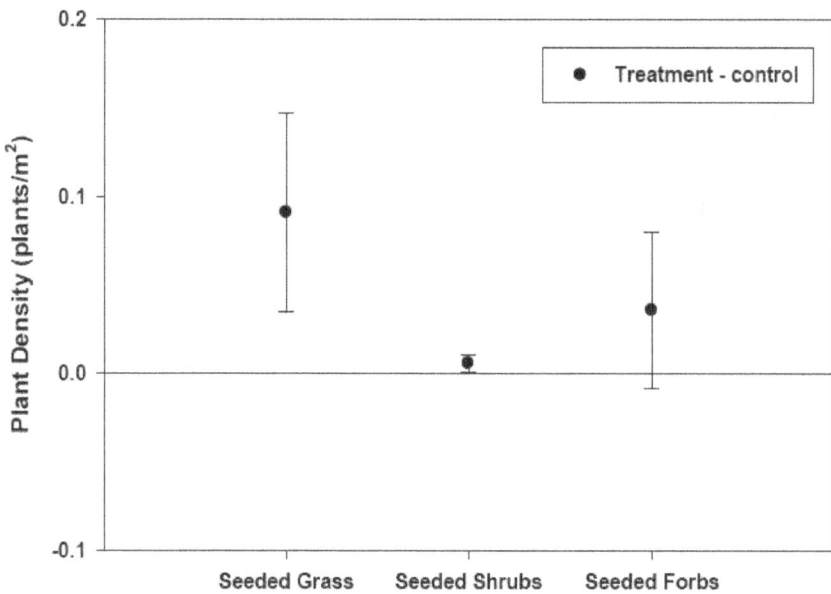

Figure 8. Confidence interval (80%) of the difference between treatment and control plots for seeded grass, shrubs, and forbs at the Cow Hollow native seeding, Oregon, 2008.

Double Mountain

The Double Mountain fire occurred on July 29, 2005, and burned a total of 17,484 acres before containment on July 30 (Bureau of Land Management, 2005b, fig. 9).

The potential plant community in the area is a shrub overstory of primarily Wyoming big sagebrush (*A. tridentata* ssp. *wyomingensis*) with deep-rooted perennial grasses such as *A. hymenoides* (Indian ricegrass), *H. comata* (needle and thread), *P. spicata* (bluebunch wheatgrass), and *A. thurberianum* (Thurber's needlegrass), along with the shallow-rooted perennial grass *P. secunda* (Sandberg bluegrass).

There were two drill seedings proposed for the Double Mountain Fire, a non-native seedmix treatment of 349 ha (863 acres) and a native seedmix treatment of 1,128 ha (2,793 acres) (table 5). At the non-native treatment, the pre-burn vegetation consisted mainly of annual grasses and forbs with some small patches of *P. secunda* (personal observation). Soils in the area consisted primarily of sandy loams. According to the Oregon State Water Resources Board (1969), soils in the area are in classification unit 60, which are described as fine-textured loams underlain by clay loams and lacustrine sediments that are weakly consolidated. The elevation at the non-native seeding treatment ranged from 785 to 902 m (2,575 to 2,960 ft).

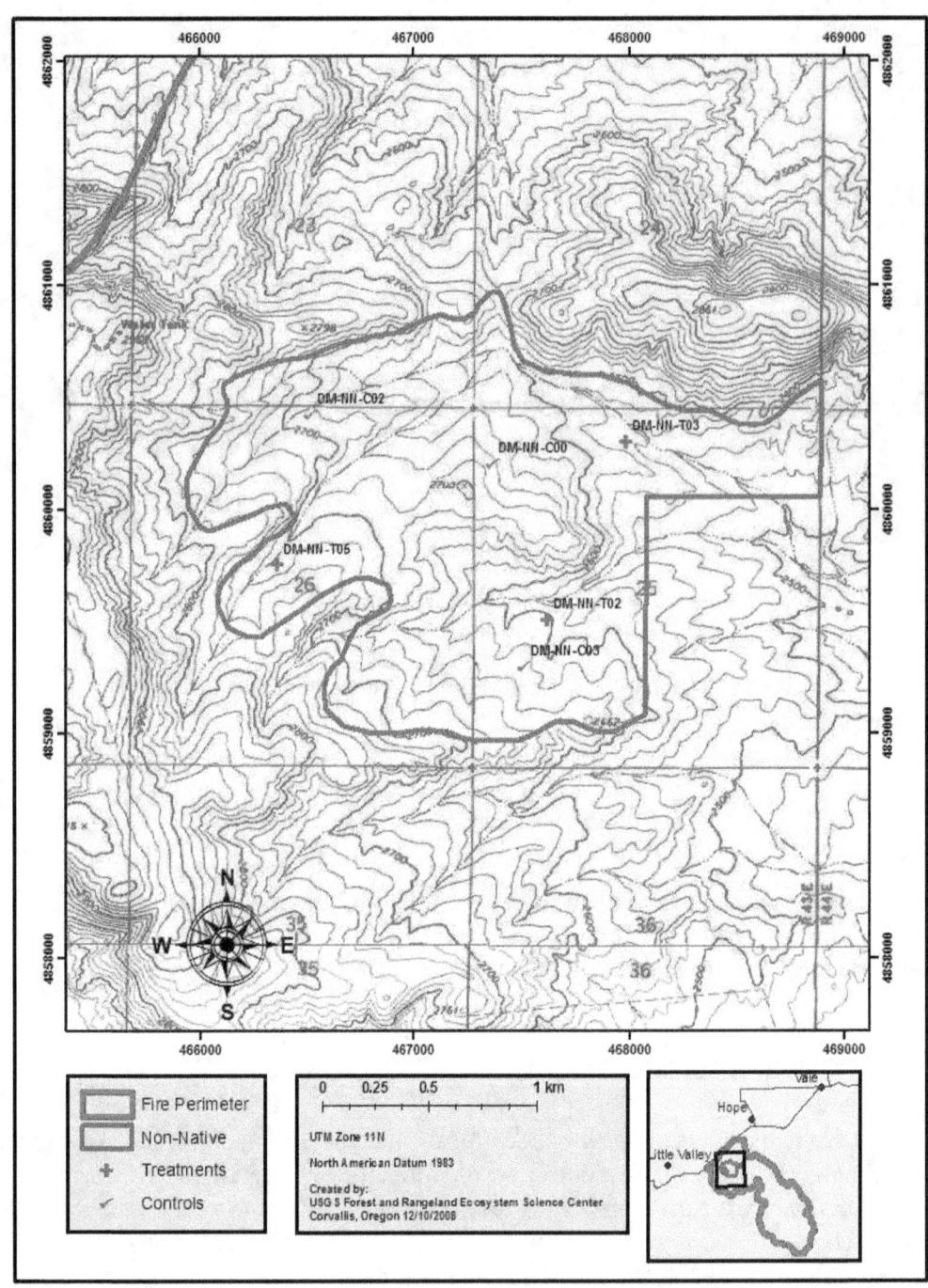

Figure 9. Location of Double Mountain non-native seeding monitoring plots, Oregon, 2006–08.

Table 5. Seed mixes at the Double Mountain native and non-native seeding, Oregon, 2005.

Native seed mix	PLS[b] (lb/acre)	Non-native seed mix	PLS[b] (lb/acre)
'Anetone' bluebunch wheatgrass (*Pseudoroegneria spicata*)	4.0	'Fairway' crested wheatgrass (*Agropyron cristatum*)	5.00
'Trailhead' basin wildrye (*Elymus cinereus*)	0.88	'Trailhead' basin wildrye (*Elymus cinereus*)	1.00
Sandberg's bluegrass (*Poa secunda*)	0.94	'Arriba' western wheatgrass (*Pascopyrum smithii*)	1.00
Squirreltail (*Elymus elymoides*)	1.00	'Ladak' alfalfa (*Medicago sativa*)	0.25
Western yarrow (*Achillea millefolium*)	0.12	Small burnet (*Sanguisorba minor*)	0.40
Annual sunflower (*Helianthus annuus*)	0.76	'Apar' Lewis flax (*Linum lewisii*)	0.10
Wyoming big sagebrush (*Artemisia tridentata* ssp. *wyomingensis*)	0.01	Wyoming big sagebrush (*Artemisia tridentata* ssp. *wyomingensis*)	0.01
		Antelope Bitterbrush (*Purshia tridentata*)	0.25
TOTAL	7.71	TOTAL	8.01

[a]Seed mixes are named native or non-native depending on the species that compose the majority of the seed mix. There is uncertainty about whether or not annual sunflower was seeded at the Double Mountain seedings. None was found during monitoring. Single quotes surround registered cultivar names for species.

[b]PLS = pure live seed.

The native seeding treatment contained much more topography and elevation range, and as a result, was much more variable than the non-native seeding treatment area. This area contained a large component of native grasses and forbs and in some areas appeared to be in good ecological condition except for the absence of a shrub component (personal observation). Soils were generally silt loams that were deeper on shallow slopes and flat areas and shallower on hills and shoulders. The range of elevation was broad, ranging from 795 to 1,037 m (2,608 to 3,402 ft).

The non-native monitoring unit consisted of slopes of up to 20%. We placed three treatment and three control plots within this monitoring unit. Likewise, the non-native seeding monitoring unit also consisted of drilled areas of 0 to 20% slopes. Due to the topography in this treatment, the monitoring unit definition eliminated more area from consideration than in the non-native seeding. Because the native treatment was larger, we also established more plots (seven treatment and four control).

Double Mountain Non-Native Seeding

Seeded grass densities at the Double Mountain non-native seeding decreased from 2.72 plants/m^2 in 2006 to 0.90 plants/m^2 in 2008 (table 6A). Very few pre-fire perennial grasses were found in the area (0.05 plants/m^2 in the treatment plots in 2008). The primary grasses establishing from seed were *A. cristatum* (0.72 plants/m^2) and *T. intermedium* (0.16 plants/m^2). Additionally, there was some establishment of seeded forbs (0.69 plants/m^2 in 2006 and 0.25 plants/m^2 in 2008), primarily *M. sativa* but also *L. lewisii* and *A. millefolium*. No seeded shrubs were found in the treatment area. *B. tectorum* densities increased nearly threefold in both control and treatment plots from 2006 to 2007, followed by a slight decrease in 2008.

Basal-gap intercept measurements from 2006 to 2008 decreased slightly in the > 200 gap-size classes and increased slightly in the 101–200 cm gap-size class (table 6B). This pattern occurred in both treatment and control plots.

Vegetation foliar cover was lower and bare ground was higher at the treatment plots in 2006 (table 6C). The relationship remained similar, but the difference between the treatment and control plots decreased in 2007 and 2008.

In 2006, there was little cover of deep-rooted perennial grass (table 6D). Shallow-rooted perennial grass cover was also low but showed an increase in the treatment plots and a decrease in the control plots from 2006 to 2008. Cover of exotic annual grasses increased in 2007 and decreased slightly in 2008. In 2006, cover of exotic annual forbs, primarily *Sisymbrium altissimum* (tall tumblemustard) was high in both control and treatment plots (37.3 and 33.6%, respectively) followed by a reduction to 0 and 2.7% in 2007, and another increase to 5.3 and 7.6% in 2008. In some areas of this treatment, *Onopordum acanthium* (Scotch cottonthistle) and *Cardaria draba* (whitetop) appear to be increasing following the fire (personal observation).

Table 6. Density of plants by functional group and *Bromus tectorum* (A), average percentage of each transect composed of basal gaps within each gap-size class (B), vegetation foliar cover, bare ground, and basal cover (C), and functional group foliar cover (D) at the Double Mountain non-native seeding, Oregon, 2006–08.

A.

Functional Group[a]	Non-native seeding treatment (plants/m²)[b]		Non-native seeding control (plants/m²)[b]	
	2006	2008	2006	2008
NS perennial grass	0.03 (0.02)	0.05 (0.02)	0.01 (0.01)	0.02 (0.02)
NS shrubs	0.00	0.00	0.00	0.00
SD perennial grass	2.72 (1.89)	0.90 (0.78)	0.08 (0.08)	0.02 (0.03)
SD shrubs	0.00	0.00	0.00	0.00
SD forbs	0.69 (0.15)	0.25 (0.13)	0.02 (0.02)	0.01 (0.01)
	2006	2007	2008	2006	2007	2008
B. tectorum	492 (131)	1461 (168)	1072 (353)	641 (89)	1705 (314)	1139 (210)

[a]NS, non-seeded; SD, seeded. Density of NS perennial grasses does not include the shallow-rooted species, *Poa secunda* or *Poa bulbosa*.

[b]Numbers in parentheses are standard errors.

B.

Gap size (cm)	Non-native seeding treatment (percent of line)			Non-native seeding control (percent of line)		
	2006	2007	2008	2006	2007	2008
25–50	0.9	1.2	1.6	2.0	1.5	1.7
51–100	2.9	3.1	4.4	1.4	2.2	3.1
101–200	4.7	5.3	9.3	5.4	6.0	8.2
>200	89.4	88.1	82.4	89.1	87.9	84.5

Table 6. Density of plants by functional group and *Bromus tectorum* (A), average percentage of each transect composed of basal gaps within each gap-size class (B), vegetation foliar cover, bare ground, and basal cover (C), and functional group foliar cover (D) at the Double Mountain non-native seeding, Oregon, 2006–08.—Continued

C.

Cover	Non-native seeding treatment (percent cover)			Non-native seeding control (percent cover)		
	2006	2007	2008	2006	2007	2008
Vegetation foliar cover	78.4	75.8	74.0	91.1	82.7	80.4
Bare ground	15.8	11.1	11.3	4.2	4.9	4.0
Basal cover	0.2	1.3	1.8	1.6	1.1	1.3

D.

Functional Group Foliar Cover[a]	Non-native treatment (percent cover)[b]			Non-native control (percent cover)[b]		
	2006	2007	2008	2006	2007	2008
DR perennial grass	0.4 (0.4)	0.9 (0.9)	1.6 (1.0)	0.2 (0.2)	0.7 (0.7)	0.7 (0.7)
SR perennial grass	4.4 (1.1)	3.8 (0.8)	8.0 (2.3)	9.1 (5.4)	6.0 (4.4)	6.7 (3.7)
Perennial forbs	1.8 (1.5)	3.8 (2.1)	2.4 (1.4)	3.3 (3.3)	6.7 (5.4)	1.3 (0.8)
Shrubs	0.0	0.0	0.0	0.0	0.0	0.0
Exotic annual grass	62.4 (5.3)	70.2 (4.3)	65.1 (9.7)	72.7 (2.4)	76.7 (7.6)	74.2 (8.7)
Exotic annual forbs	33.6 (12.0)	2.7 (0.8)	7.6 (3.0)	37. 3 (1.9)	0.0	5.3 (1.4)
Litter	43.6 (1.5)	73. 6 (0.6)	74.7 (6.2)	82.0 (7.1)	84.7 (6.7)	89.3 (3.)

[a]DR, deep-rooted; SR, shallow-rooted; Exotic annual grasses primarily *B. tectorum*.

[b]Numbers in parentheses are standard errors.

Double Mountain Non-Native Seeding Conclusions

Final densities of seeded grasses at the Double Mountain non-native seeding were less than the target density of 5 plants/m^2 and highly variable (fig. 10). Established perennial grass density is estimated to be between 0 and 2.36 plants/m^2 with a mean of 0.90 plants/m^2. Because the confidence interval overlapped zero, the treatment was not statistically different than control plots in terms of established perennial grasses. However, the seeding did increase the number of perennial grass plants (by an estimated 9,000 plants/ha) in the area. Due to the low number of plots and the patchiness of seedling establishment, the 80% confidence interval for seeded perennial grasses was large.

At this seeding, the drill created large furrows in the sandy soils, which, in the first year following the fire, seemed to increase bare ground in treatment areas. These furrows did not increase the overall density or cover of exotic annual grasses over the 3-year monitoring period and may have aided the establishment of perennial grasses by creating an adequate seedbed.

Double Mountain Native Seeding

The Double Mountain native seeding consists of several polygons on the southern end of the area affected by the Double Mountain fire (fig. 11).

The density of perennial seeded grasses in 2008 at the Double Mountain native seeding was the highest of the four 2005 fires. Although initial densities were lower than that recorded at the Keeney Pass native seeding treatment in 2006, there was less mortality at the Double Mountain native seeding, leading to higher establishment by 2008. There was an estimated 3.86 seeded perennial grass plants/m^2 in 2006 and 1.74 plants/m^2 in 2008 (table 7A). The majority of seeded grasses established were *P. spicata*. There was very little establishment of seeded forbs and shrubs (less than 0.01 plants/m^2). *B. tectorum* densities increased from 2006 to 2007 and leveled off in 2008 in both treatment and control plots.

Basal-gap intercept measurements were similar between treatment and control plots with most gaps in the > 200 cm gap-size class (table 7B). Other gap-size classes stayed largely the same; however, there was a slight decrease in the number of gaps in the 51–100 cm gap-size class in control plots.

Vegetation foliar cover, bare ground, and basal cover showed the same patterns in treatment and control plots during monitoring (table 7C). From 2006 to 2008, there was an increase in vegetation foliar cover in the treatment and control. During this time, bare ground decreased by approximately one-half in both treatments.

Deep-rooted perennial grass cover increased slightly in the treatment and control plots from 2006 to 2008 (table 7D). Shallow-rooted perennial grass cover showed a slight increase in treatment plots and a larger increase in control plots. One control plot was primarily responsible for this trend due to a large increase in *P. secunda* cover in 2008. Exotic annual-grass cover increased during 2006-2008 in both the treatment and control plots; however, this effect was more pronounced in the treatment plots. Exotic annual forbs generally decreased from an initial flush in 2006, and litter increased in all plots during the monitoring period.

Double Mountain Native Seeding Conclusions

The native seeding at Double Mountain did not meet the objective of 5 plants/m^2, but there was substantial establishment of seeded grasses. Initial plant densities were lower than 5 plants/m^2 in 2006, and subsequent mortality from low precipitation in 2007 and 2008 reduced the densities further. Seeded perennial grass density was estimated to be between 0.95 and 2.53 plant/m^2 with a mean of 1.74 plants/m^2 (fig. 12). Due to the variable nature of the pre-fire ecological conditions, greater and more complex topography, and the wider elevation range at this treatment, there was substantial patchiness in seedling establishment. Some plots had large numbers of establishing seedlings whereas others had dense patches of *P. secunda* that seemed to preclude seedling establishment. High initial densities of exotic annual grasses at some plots also may have severely reduced treatment seedling establishment due to competition. There also were areas where it appeared that drill rows and subsequent seedling establishment were dependent on the absence of dense *P. secunda* (fig. 13).

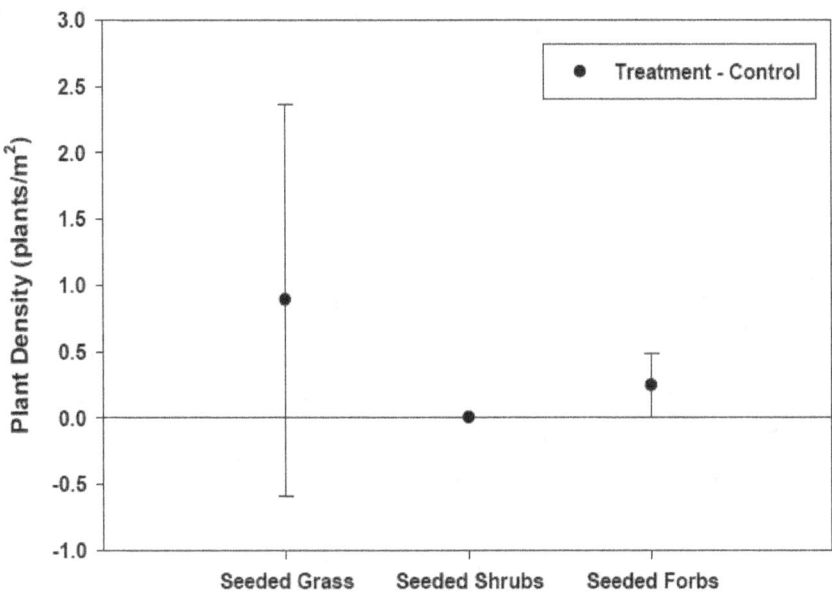

Figure 10. Confidence interval (80%) of the difference between treatment and control plots for densities of seeded grasses, shrubs, and forbs at the Double Mountain non-native seeding, Oregon, 2008.

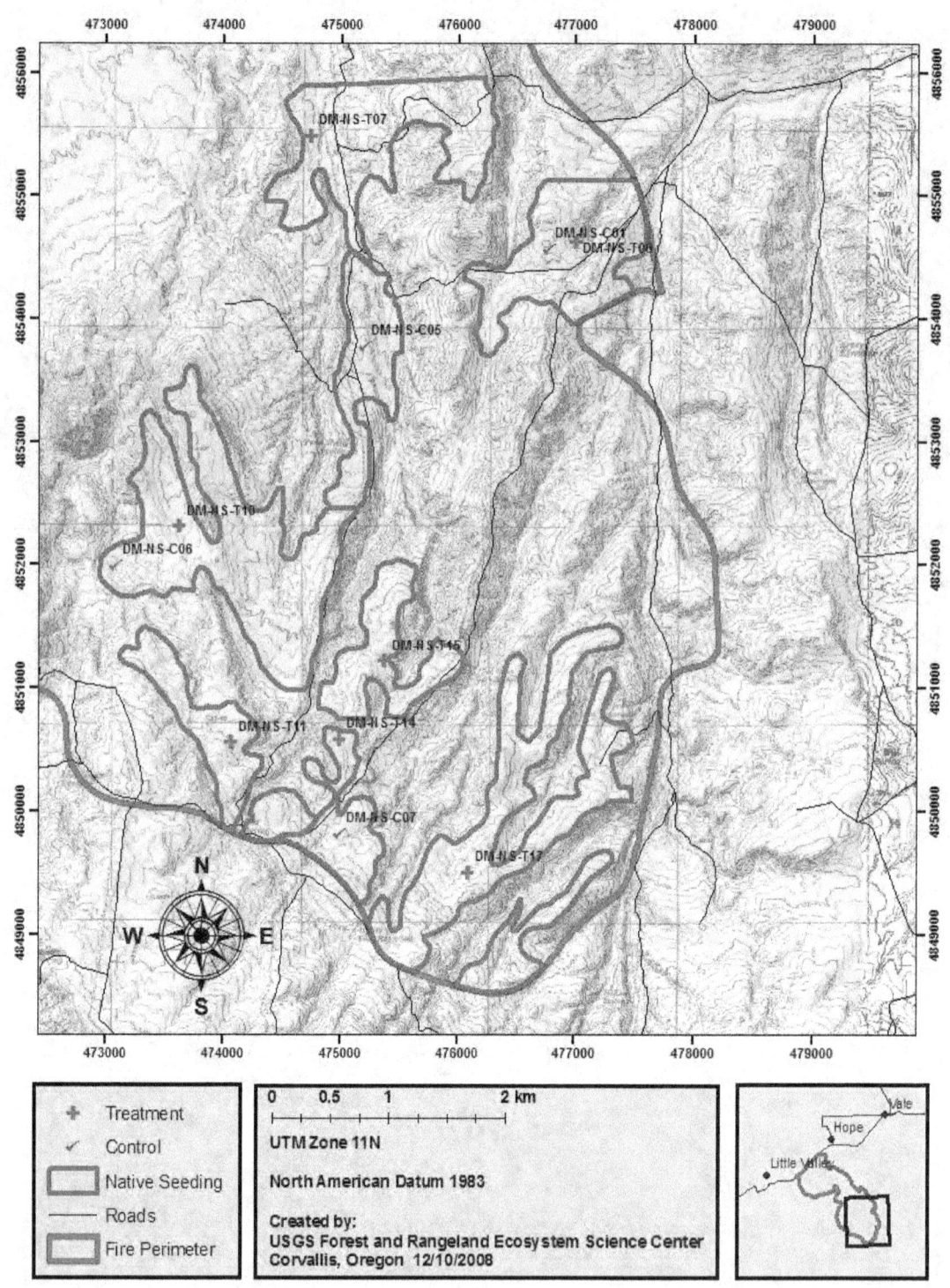

Figure 11. Location of monitoring plots at the Double Mountain native seeding treatment, Oregon, 2006–08.

Table 7. Density of plants by functional group and *Bromus tectorum* (A), average percentage of each transect composed of basal gaps within each gap-size class (B), vegetation foliar cover, bare ground, and basal cover (C), and functional group foliar cover (D) at the Double Mountain native seeding, Oregon, 2006–08.

A.

Functional group[a]	Native seeding treatment (plants/m²)[b]		Native seeding control (plants/m²)[b]	
	2006	**2008**	**2006**	**2008**
NS perennial grass	1.19 (0.47)	1.39 (0.62)	0.89 (0.59)	1.10 (0.80)
NS shrubs	0.00 (0.00)	0.00 (0.00)	0.01 (0.01)	0.01 (0.01)
SD perennial grass	3.857 (1.296)	1.74 (0.50)	0.05 (0.05)	0.00
SD shrubs	0.01 (0.01)	0.00 (0.00)	0.00	0.00
SD forbs	0.03 (0.03)	0.00 (0.00)	0.00	0.00

	2006	**2007**	**2008**	**2006**	**2007**	**2008**
B. tectorum	264 (83)	611 (194)	562 (176)	313 (183)	529 (198)	540 (257)

B.

Gap Size (cm)	Native Seeding Treatment (percent of line)			Native Seeding Control (percent of line)		
	2006	**2007**	**2008**	**2006**	**2007**	**2008**
25-50	13.5	12.7	11.7	13.2	12.6	14.2
51–100	13.8	14.9	12.8	14.3	12.1	10.6
101–200	16.0	12.5	14.4	10.7	11.9	12.1
>200	40.8	40.2	45.5	45.7	42.1	43.3

C.

Cover	Native seeding treatment (percent cover)			Native seeding control (percent cover)		
	2006	**2007**	**2008**	**2006**	**2007**	**2008**
Vegetation foliar cover	57.2	57.9	64.8	59.5	56.3	66.0
Bare ground	37.0	24.2	17.7	33.0	23.2	17.0
Basal cover	4.4	6.8	6.9	4.0	6.2	8.7

Table 7. Density of plants by functional group and *Bromus tectorum* (A), average percentage of each transect composed of basal gaps within each gap-size class (B), vegetation foliar cover, bare ground, and basal cover (C), and functional group foliar cover (D) at the Double Mountain native seeding, Oregon, 2006–08.—Continued

D.

Functional Group Foliar Cover[a]	Native seeding treatment (percent cover)[b]			Native seeding control (percent cover)[b]		
	2006	2007	2008	2006	2007	2008
DR perennial grass	7.8 (2.2)	12.6 (3.5)	11.1 (3.3)	5.8 (4.8)	7.0 (5.3)	7.7 (6.8)
SR perennial grass	19.1 (5.3)	18.6 (5.4)	21.7 (5.1)	23.5 (9.0)	19.2 (7.2)	28.5 (9.5)
Perennial forbs	3.1 (0.9)	2.9 (0.8)	2.0 (0.4)	1.1 (0.8)	2.5 (0.9)	2.2 (0.8)
Shrubs	0.2 (0.2)	0.1 (0.1)	0.3 (0.3)	0.0	0.3 (0.2)	0.2 (0.2)
Exotic annual grass	28.6 (7.6)	32.0 (6.8)	39.7 (8.9)	32.5 (12.3)	33.3 (13.0)	34.8 (13.9)
Exotic annual forbs	8.2 (3.7)	2.5 (1.4)	2.8 (1.3)	5.2 (2.9)	1.8 (0.7)	2.3 (1.0)
Litter	19.9 (4.6)	50.2 (4.7)	60.0 (2.1)	26.7 (6.8)	54.5 (10.4)	60.3 (7.4)

[a]DR, deep-rooted; SR, shallow-rooted; Exotic annual grasses primarily *B. tectorum*.

[b]Numbers in parentheses are standard errors.

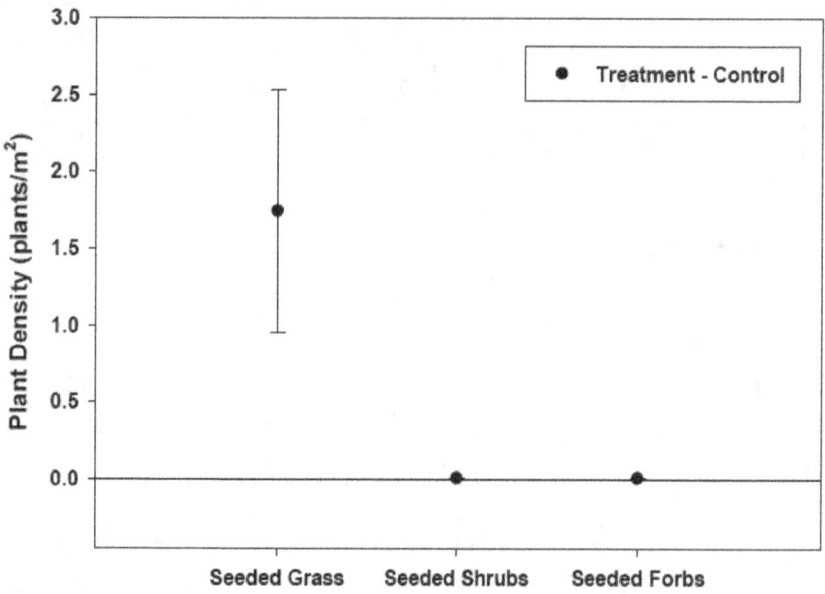

Figure 12. Confidence interval (80%) of the difference between the treatment and control for seeded grasses, shrubs, and forbs at the Double Mountain native seeding, Oregon, 2008.

Figure 13. Photograph of establishing seedlings in an area where _ _secu___ was less dense prior to seeding or was displaced during seeding (at right) and an adjacent area of dense _ _secu___ with little seedling establishment (left middle).

Farewell Bend

The Farewell Bend fire was ignited by lightning on July 28, 2005, and burned approximately 3,418 acres of BLM land before containment on July 29 (fig. 14).

The potential plant community in the area of the Farewell Bend fire is a shrub overstory of primarily Wyoming big sagebrush (_A. tridentata_ ssp. _wyomingensis_) with deep rooted perennial grasses such as _P. spicata_ (bluebunch wheatgrass), _A. thurberianum_ (Thurber's needlegrass), and _Festuca idahoensis_ (Idaho Fescue) along with the shallow-rooted perennial grass _P. secunda_ (Sandberg bluegrass) (NRCS, 1997). Some areas are close to Benson Creek and species such as chokecherry (_Prunus_) and Syringa (_Philadelphus lewisii_) can be found in these areas, as well as more mesic plants within the creek itself.

Soils at the Farewell Bend are clayey (clay loam to clay) and have a subsurface layer high in smectitic clay (27–50%) with a moderate to high linear extensibility (3–8.9%). This high clay content causes cracking of the soil surface due to shrinking and swelling of the soils during wet-dry cycles. As a result of this soil surface cracking, bunchgrasses tend to be either semi-rhizomatous or broken apart by the shrink-swell cycle (fig. 15). This shrink-swell cycle also tends to obscure the drill rows, which are useful as a visual guide when searching for seedlings during monitoring. The rhizomatous nature of the vegetation in this area makes it difficult to consistently identify the boundaries of individuals as well as determine the difference between recently established seeded plants and pre-existing plants.

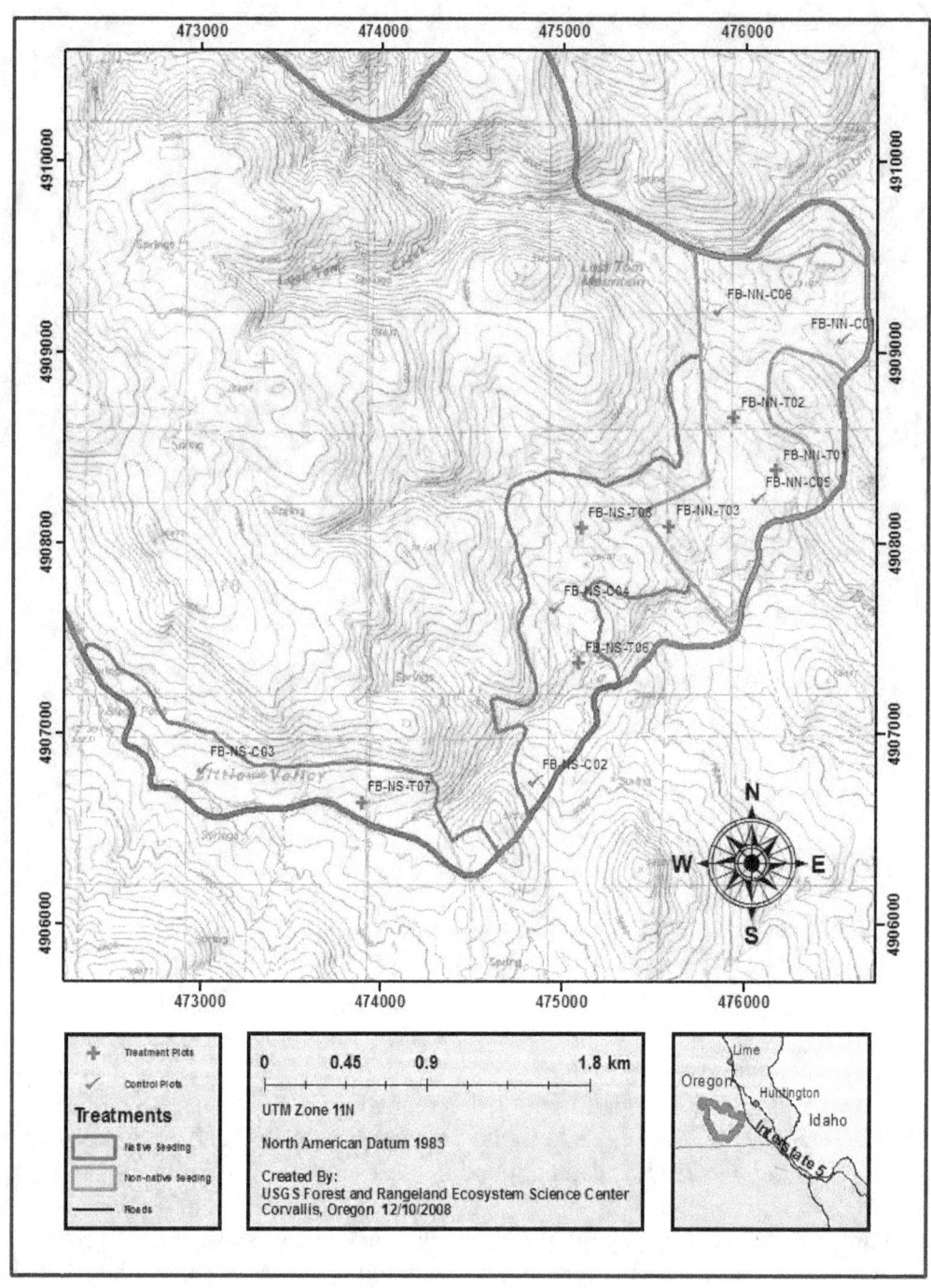

Figure 14. Location of Farewell Bend monitoring plots, Oregon, 2006-08.

Figure 15. Soil surface conditions and rhizomatous *Pseudoroegneria spicata* at the Farewell Bend burned area, Oregon.

Two seedmixes, one composed of native species, and the other mostly non-native species, were drill-seeded in the Farewell Bend burned area in 2005 (table 8). The non-native seedmix was seeded over 116 ha (288 acres) and the native seedmix was drilled on 166 ha (412 acres) of the burned area. A portion of the non-native treatment was a previous crested wheatgrass seeding, however, pre-fire vegetation at both treatments consisted primarily of native perennial grasses dominated by semi-rhizomatous *P. spicata* and *P. secunda*. In some areas, *P. bulbosa* had replaced *P. secunda* as the dominant shallow-rooted grass. The elevation of the two treatments ranged from 820 to 940 m (2,690 to 3,083 ft).

Two monitoring units were defined as those areas that were drill seeded between 0 and 20% slopes for each of the seedmixes. Quantitative goals were to establish 5 seeded plants/m^2. There were three exotic annual grasses present, *B. tectorum*, *Bromus hordeaceus* (soft brome), and *Taeniatherum caput-medusae* (medusahead). Due to the small size of treatment areas, there were only three treatment and control plots established in each treatment area.

Table 8. Seed mix at the Farewell Bend non-native and native seedings, Oregon.

Non-native seed mix	PLS[b] (lb/acre)	Native seed mix	PLS[b] (lb/acre)
'Hycrest' wheatgrass (*Agropyron cristatum*)	4.0	'Magnar' basin wildrye (*Elymus cinereus*)	4.0
'Ephraim' crested wheatgrass *Agropyron cristatum*	3.0	'Schwendimar' thickspike wheatgrass (*Elymus lanceolatus*)	4.6
'Luna' pubescent wheatgrass (*Thinopyron intermedium*)	2.0	Blue wildrye (*Elymus glaucus*)	0.8
Sandberg's bluegrass (*Poa secunda*)	1.0	Canby bluegrass (*Poa secunda*)	1.0
Basin big sagebrush (*Artemisia tridentata* ssp. *vaseyana*)	0.2	Basin big sagebrush (*Artemisia tridentata* ssp. *vaseyana*)	0.2
TOTAL	10.2	TOTAL	10.6

[a]Seedmixes are named native or non-native depending on the species that compose the majority of the seedmix. Common sunflower was seeded at the Farewell Bend burned area but its rate was not known. Single quotes surround registered cultivar names for species.

[b]PLS = pure live seed

Farewell Bend Non-Native Seeding

Resprouting native perennial grasses accounted for 5.00 plants/m^2 in the treatment and 6.80 plants/m^2 in the control plots in 2008 (table 9A). In 2006, there was an estimated 5.62 seeded perennial grass plants/m^2, which decreased to 0.42 plants/m^2 by 2008. Establishing seeded plants were primarily *A. cristatum* (0.35 plants/m^2) with low densities of *E. lanceolatus* (0.05 plants/m^2). Seeded shrub (*A. tridentata* ssp. *vaseyana*) density was estimated to be 0.14 plants/m^2 in 2008. In a few areas that had sagebrush prior to the fire, there were patches of naturally occurring sagebrush seedlings. These were defined as non-seeded for monitoring purposes, but there may have been some seeded plants in these areas. Densities of exotic annuals increased from 2006 to 2007, as it did in all other seedings, and then decreased in 2008, although not to 2006 levels.

Basal-gap intercept measurements in the 25–50 cm gap-size class were similar from 2006 to 2008 (table 9B). In treatment plots, gaps in the 51–100 cm gap-size class increased from 17.3 to 26.0%, and there was no corresponding increase in control plots. At the same time, there was a decrease in the percentage of transects in the 101–200 and >200 cm gap-size classes.

Bare ground decreased in treatment plots and remained constant at control plots during the monitoring period (table 9C). Vegetation foliar cover increased slightly from 2006 to 2007 and then decreased in 2008 at both treatment and control plots. Basal cover generally increased from 2006 to 2008 in treatment and control plots.

Functional group foliar cover of resprouting shallow-rooted grasses (primarily *P. bulbosa*) at treatment plots showed a marked increase from 2006 to 2007, followed by a decrease in 2008 (table 9D). Control plots followed a similar trend except that cover was the same in both 2007 and 2008. Exotic annual grass cover increased in 2007 and decreased in 2008 in both treatment and control plots. Cover of exotic annual forbs increased by small amounts in 2007 and 2008.

Table 9. Density of plants by functional group and *Bromus tectorum* (A), average percentage of each transect composed of basal gaps within each gap-size class (B), vegetation foliar cover, bare ground, and basal cover (C), and functional group foliar cover (D) at the Farewell Bend non-native seeding, Oregon, 2006–08.

A.

Functional group[a]	Non-native seeding treatment (plants/m²)[b]		Non-native seeding control (plants/m²)[b]	
	2006	2008	2006	2008
NS perennial grass	5.05 (1.01)	5.00 (0.92)	6.26 (2.75)	6.80 (2.94)
NS shrubs	0.00	0.01 (0.01)	0.00 (0.00)	0.14 (0.12)
SD perennial grass	5.62 (3.99)	0.42 (0.12)	0.02 (0.01)	0.00
SD shrubs	0.155 (0.109)	0.128 (0.120)	0.078 (0.044)	0.000

	2006	2007	2008	2006	2007	2008
Exotic annual grass	115 (48)	379 (128)	233 (58)	151 (100)	650 (177)	415 (192)

[a]NS, non-seeded; SD, seeded. Density of NS perennial grasses does not include the shallow-rooted species, *Poa secunda* or *Poa bulbosa*.

[b]Numbers in parentheses are standard errors.

B.

Gap size (cm)	Non-native seeding treatment (percent of line)			Non-native seeding control (percent of line)		
	2006	2007	2008	2006	2007	2008
25-50	14.0	16.1	17.1	13.4	14.1	15.1
51–100	17.3	17.2	26.0	14.7	13.3	13.7
101–200	19.3	16.5	13.5	12.0	13.0	13.9
>200	21.5	13.8	14.3	36.0	30.4	28.8

C.

Cover	Non-native seeding treatment (percent cover)			Non-native seeding control (percent cover)		
	2006	2007	2008	2006	2007	2008
Vegetation foliar cover	61.7	68.9	55.1	68.6	70.0	60.4
Bare ground	26.1	11.3	16.5	16.2	13.1	15.1
Basal cover	4.4	10.4	7.6	4.7	8.7	8.9

Table 9. Density of plants by functional group and *Bromus tectorum* (A), average percentage of each transect composed of basal gaps within each gap-size class (B), vegetation foliar cover, bare ground, and basal cover (C), and functional group foliar cover (D) at the Farewell Bend non-native seeding, Oregon, 2006–08.—Continued

D.

Functional Group Foliar Cover[a]	Non-native seeding treatment (percent cover)[b]			Non-native seeding control (percent cover)[b]		
	2006	2007	2008	2006	2007	2008
DR perennial grass	13.6 (5.2)	16.7 (9.3)	14.0 (4.2)	16.9 (7.7)	18.4 (7.1)	13.8 (3.6)
SR perennial grass	19.1 (7.1)	29.6 (8.9)	23.3 (4.9)	17.6 (10.8)	22.0 (10.9)	22.0 (11.6)
Perennial forbs	11.1 (3.4)	6.9 (3.9)	6.0 (3.0)	8.2 (1.4)	8.7 (3.0)	8.7 (3.5)
Shrubs	0.0	0.2 (0.2)	0.2 (0.2)	0.0	0.2 (0.2)	1.6 (0.4)
Exotic annual grass	26.4 (6.1)	34.2 (8.3)	18.9 (6.5)	38.2 (17.5)	44.9 (20.6)	26.4 (11.4)
Exotic annual forbs	1.1 (0.4)	1.6 (1.2)	3.3 (2.3)	1.1 (0.4)	1.6 (0.2)	2.7 (1.3)
Litter	24.4 (4.8)	59.8 (4.1)	65.7 (3.7)	42.2 (2.3)	55.1 (7.5)	60.4 (7.3)

[a]DR, deep-rooted; SR, shallow-rooted; Exotic annual grasses includes *B. tectorum*, *T. caput-medusae*, and *B. hordeaceous* which are all present at Farewell Bend

[b]Numbers in parentheses are standard errors.

Farewell Bend Non-Native Seeding Conclusions

The non-native seeding of the Farewell Bend burned area did not meet the quantitative target objective of 5 plants/m^2. Seeded grass densities at the Farewell Bend non-native seeding were estimated to be between 0.19 and 0.64 with a mean of 0.42 plants/m^2 (fig. 16). This is equivalent to an estimated 4,180 plants/ha.

At this site, there was considerable natural recovery of existing grasses and perennial forbs, which most likely provided substantial competition to seeded species. The high density of plants that survived the fire in the non-native treatment (5.0 to 6.8 plants/m^2) is due primarily to the previous successful *A. cristatum* seeding, which is very dense in some locations.

The large changes in gap percentages at treatment plots may be partially due to the mechanical action of the drill seeding which would be expected to increase the percentage of transects in larger gap sizes. Furthermore, the cracking and shifting clay soils may have increased variability of the basal-gap intercept data by physically moving plants between years.

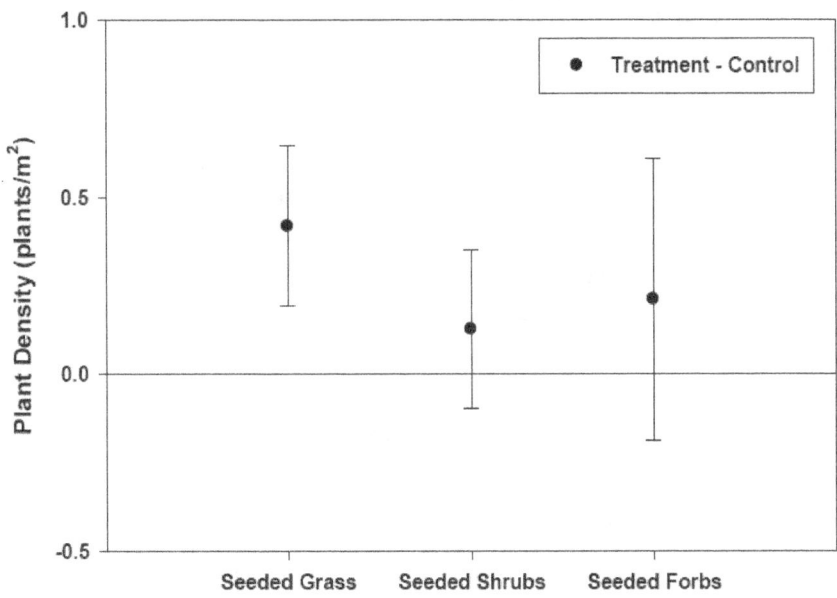

Figure 16. Confidence interval (80%) of the difference between the treatment and control at the Farewell Bend non-native seeding, Oregon, 2008.

Farewell Bend Native Seeding

Density of seeded perennial grasses decreased from 2.22 to 0.44 plants/m² from 2006 to 2008 (table 10A). Seeded shrubs (*A. tridentata*) decreased from 0.54 to 0.20 plants/m² during the monitoring period. Exotic annual grass densities increased at both the control and treatment plots in 2007, but then decreased in 2008 for the control plots only.

Basal-gap intercept measurements at treatment plots decreased in the >200 cm gap class from 53.1 to 37.2%, whereas control plots decreased from 38.8 to 31.6% (table 10B). Average percentage of lines occupied by the remaining three gap classes showed little change during the monitoring period.

Vegetation foliar cover and basal cover increased in both treatment and control plots from 2006 to 2008 (table 10C). Simultaneously, bare ground cover decreased substantially in both treatments (to approximately 25% of 2006 levels).

Cover of perennial grasses increased from 2006 to 2008 in treatment and control plots (table 10D). Cover of perennial native forbs was higher at the Farewell Bend native seeding than at any of the other burned areas. Cover of exotic annual forbs was low but increasing by 2008. As with other burned areas, litter increased steadily from 2006 to 2008 as biomass accumulated after the fire.

Table 10. Density of plants by functional group and *Bromus tectorum* (A), average percentage of each transect composed of basal gaps within each gap-size class (B), vegetation foliar cover, bare ground, and basal cover (C), and functional group foliar cover (D) at the Farewell Bend native seeding, Oregon, 2006–08.

A.

Functional group[a]	Native seeding treatment (plants/m²)[b]		Native seeding control (plants/m²)[b]	
	2006	2008	2006	2008
NS perennial grass	2.01 (0.66)	1.46 (0.83)	1.07 (0.13)	1.33 (0.70)
NS shrubs	0.06 (0.04)	0.08 (0.05)	0.17 (0.13)	0.11 (0.02)
SD perennial grass	2.22 (0.19)	0.44 (0.12)	0.02 (0.02)	0.00
SD shrubs	0.54 (0.43)	0.20 (0.17)	0.00	0.00
SD forbs	0.01 (0.01)	0.15 (0.13)	0.00	0.00

	2006	2007	2008	2006	2007	2008
Exotic annual grass	243 (49)	646 (180)	658 (247)	261 (83)	739 (187)	333 (178)

[a]NS, non-seeded; SD, seeded. Density of NS perennial grasses does not include the shallow-rooted species, *Poa secunda* or *Poa bulbosa*.

[b]Numbers in parentheses are standard errors.

B.

Gap Size (cm)	Native seeding treatment (percent of line)			Native seeding control (percent of line)		
	2006	2007	2008	2006	2007	2008
25-50	9.9	9.1	13.1	10.8	7.8	11.3
51–100	12.9	15.0	14.3	15.2	10.1	11.0
101–200	12.8	14.3	18.6	12.2	14.2	11.7
>200	53.1	48.9	37.2	38.8	38.4	31.6

C.

Cover	Native seeding treatment (percent cover)			Native seeding control (percent cover)		
	2006	2007	2008	2006	2007	2008
Vegetation foliar cover	63.8	68.4	74.2	67.5	67.3	80.0
Bare ground	25.6	10.7	6.4	19.8	11.8	4.9
Basal cover	2.0	6.2	7.6	4.8	5.1	11.3

Table 10. Density of plants by functional group and *Bromus tectorum* (A), average percentage of each transect composed of basal gaps within each gap-size class (B), vegetation foliar cover, bare ground, and basal cover (C), and functional group foliar cover (D) at the Farewell Bend native seeding, Oregon, 2006–08.—Continued

D.

Functional Group Foliar Cover[a]	Native seeding treatment (percent cover)[b]			Native seeding control (percent cover)[b]		
	2006	2007	2008	2006	2007	2008
DR perennial grass	9.6 (4.9)	10.7 (5.4)	15.3 (6.0)	2.7 (1.3)	3.1 (0.8)	7.3 (3.2)
SR perennial grass	8.7 (5.2)	15.3 (7.6)	20.2 (7.3)	22.7 (12.4)	23.6 (14.5)	37.6 (20.9)
Perennial forbs	17.8 (7.8)	10.7 (2.7)	18.0 (2.4)	20.9 (6.9)	12.9 (10.2)	27.8 (15.4)
Shrubs	0.4 (0.4)	0.9 (0.4)	1.6 (1.6)	2.0 (0.8)	2.4 (1.4)	3.6 (1.2)
Exotic annual grass	36.7 (7.2)	55.8 (7.6)	39.8 (12.7)	29.1 (5.8)	44.9 (1.4)	29.1 (15.9)
Exotic annual forbs	3.1 (1.6)	2.4 (1.4)	8.0 (3.7)	3.1 (0.9)	2.7 (2.0)	8.2 (4.6)
Litter	21.6 (2.1)	66.4 (2.2)	73.6 (4.5)	21.6 (6.8)	59.6 (9.0)	69.8 (3.2)

[a]DR, deep-rooted; SR, shallow-rooted; Exotic annual grasses includes *B. tectorum*, *T. caput-medusae*, and *B. hordeaceous* which are all present at Farewell Bend

[b]Numbers in parentheses are standard errors.

Farewell Bend Native Seeding Conclusions

The Farewell Bend native seeding did not meet the 5 plants/m^2 quantitative objective. The density of perennial grasses established by drill seeding was estimated to be between 0.23 and 0.67 plants/m^2 with a mean of 0.44 plants/m^2 (fig. 17). This is equivalent to an estimated 4,400 plants/ha established as a result of the seeding by 2008. In addition, there was a large amount of natural recovery following the fire at this site.

Time Requirements

Average times required to perform the line-point intercept, basal-gap intercept, and quadrat density procedures along one transect were 10.4, 11.6, and 19.3 minutes, respectively. Median times were slightly lower with 9, 11, and 16.3 minutes required for the line-point intercept, basal-gap intercept and quadrat density, respectively. The median time required to accomplish each procedure at one plot with three transects was 54 minutes for the line-point intercept procedure, 66 minutes for basal- gap intercept and 49 minutes for quadrat density (fig. 18). Time estimates were based on 133 line-point intercept, 138 basal-gap intercept, and 66 quadrat density transects. Belt density was not measured but usually requires less time than the other three procedures.

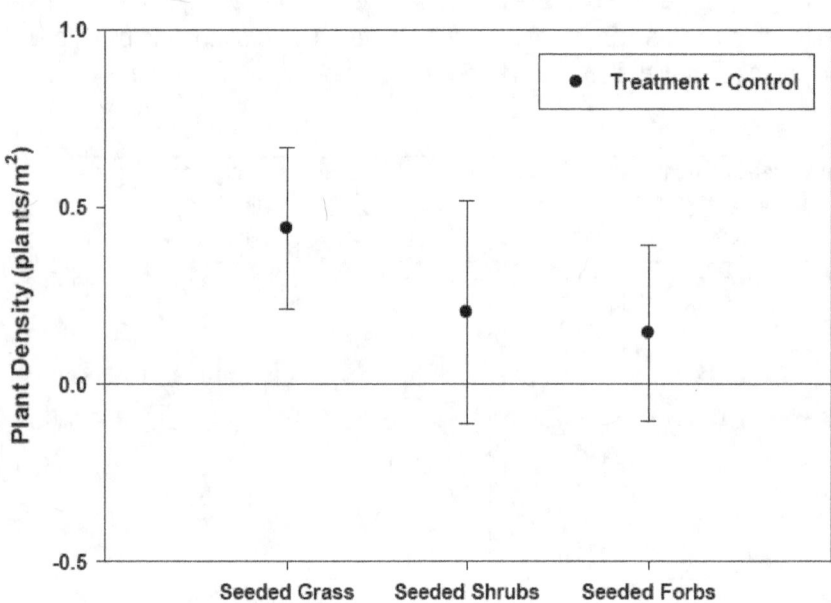

Figure 17. Confidence interval (80%) of the difference between treatment and control plots at the Farewell Bend native seeding, Oregon, 2008.

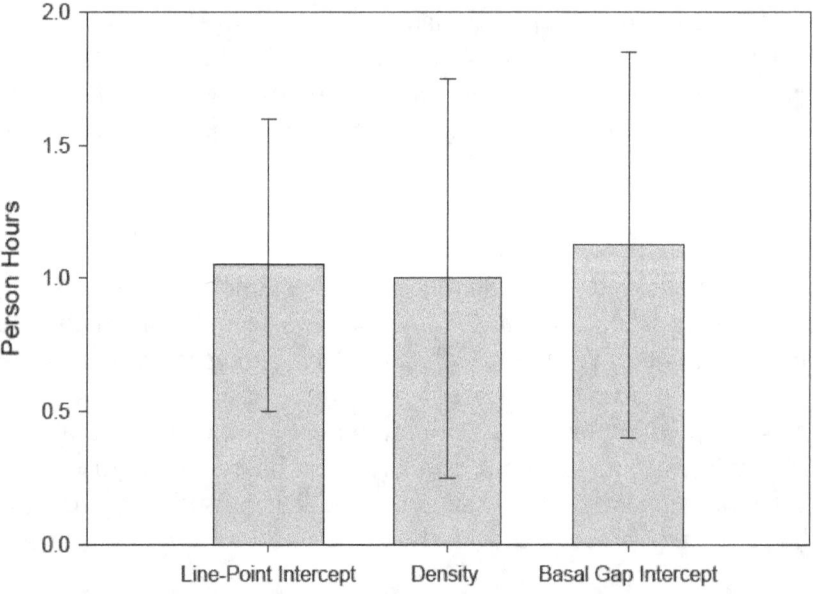

Figure 18. Median person-hours to perform each quantitative procedure on one plot (three 50-m transects). Line-point intercept and basal-gap intercept measurements require two people; density measurements require one person. Bars are maximum and minimum person-hours required.

For line-point intercept, maximum times occurred in plant communities with high cover, high diversity, and where some plants were unknown. Maximum time requirements for the basal-gap intercept procedure were a result of dense mats of *P. secunda* with high densities of other plants. Density transects with the longest time requirements occurred in areas with high plant densities where determination of individuals was difficult and the size class of each plant needed to be determined. Situations that required these maximum times were uncommon, with the exception of the dense mat of *P. secunda*, which may be common depending on the pre-burn vegetation of the area. The median time required to complete the three techniques on each plot is 2.8 hours (not including plot setup and travel time). Additional time is necessary to set up each plot in the first year of monitoring, and this usually requires 30 to 60 minutes to locate and place transects and to record pertinent plot information (slope, aspect, and soils information).

Observer Comparisons

In 2006, treatments on the Keeney Pass and Farewell Bend fires were monitored using three teams to determine variation in data among different observers. At each plot, the first team established the plot and conducted the line-point intercept, density, and basal-gap intercept procedures. Within 1–2 days, the second and third teams located the plot and also performed the procedures at that time.

Coefficients of variation for cover, density and basal-gap intercept were calculated using the standard deviation of the three teams divided by the average of the three teams multiplied by 100. Comparisons of cover and density estimates between different observers generally indicated that monitoring results were similar for common plant functional groups, but estimates varied more widely for the less common functional groups (table 11). For example, pre-existing perennial grass plants were common in treatment and control plots and the coefficient of variation among observers for cover and density were low (5.8 and 16.8%, respectively). Both seeded and non-seeded shrubs were uncommon and patchy, resulting in high coefficients of variation among observers for cover (124%) and density (82.8% for non-seeded and 70% for seeded shrubs). The Coefficients of variation for all basal-gap intercept classes were low between observers, indicating this technique is highly repeatable.

In general, coefficients of variation for seeded species were fairly high because at these seedings, seedling establishment was patchy. Treatments that result in high plant densities are expected to have lower variation between observers.

Table 11. Coefficients of variation between three sets of observers at the Farewell Bend and Keeney Pass burned areas.

Cover	Coefficient of variation (%)	Density	Coefficient of variation (%)	Basal-Gapintercept	Coefficient of variation (%)
Canopy Cover	4.3	Perennial Grasses	16.8	25-50 cm	34.2
Bare Ground	14.1	Shrubs	82.8	51-100 cm	22.1
Basal Cover	41.5	Seeded Grasses	78.1	101–200 cm	13.3
Perennial Grass	5.8	Seeded Forbs	85.0	> 200 cm	16.8
Shrubs	124.0	Seeded Shrubs	70.0		
Forbs	39	Annual Grasses	17.0		

Performance of Design Elements

Objectives

Overall, quantitative objectives are valuable parts of monitoring initial success of post-fire seedings; however, they require adaptation for specific situations or areas and adjustments as more information becomes available. Appropriate quantitative objectives for a particular parameter at a post-fire project are often unknown and setting these objectives is an adaptive process. Initially, these objectives may seem arbitrary because there are no quantitative data from past projects to use as a guide. However, as objectives are re-evaluated at the end of each project to determine if they were appropriate, this information can be used to inform future projects.

Understanding the potential of a particular area to reach a certain level of density or cover of desirable plant species is not an exact science. For example, ecological site descriptions produced by the Natural Resources Conservation Service provide information on species composition but do not specify cover or density of species that typically occur in these locations (Society for Range Management, 1999). As a result, areas that occur on similar ecological sites may differ in the amount of vegetation resulting from fewer individual plants of the same size, or from the same density of plants, but each plant is smaller, or both fewer and smaller plants. These variations of cover, density, and spatial arrangements of plants have significant impacts on what quantitative objectives are appropriate for a particular post-fire rehabilitation site.

In this report , the original density objective for seeded grasses of 5 plants/m^2 (50,000 plants/ha) or about 0.5 plants/ft^2 is considered at the lower end of a good seeding for sites that receive 28 to 33 cm (11-13 in.) of precipitation annually (Vallentine, 1971). The four 2005 Vale burns discussed in this report are on the lower end of that precipitation range, with the exception of Farewell Bend, and seedings at these burned areas resulted in lower densities than those suggested by Vallentine (1971). Therefore, the original objective of 5 plants/m^2 will need to be refined over time using data from multiple projects occurring in different years with variable timing and amount of precipitation. Additionally, densities of *B. tectorum* from 2005 to 2008 were much higher than the original density objective of 100 plants/m^2. *Bromus tectorum* exhibited high annual variation as a result of both disturbance (fire, drill seeding) and climate (wet year followed by two drought years). As a result, density of *B. tectorum* may be difficult to use as an objective, at least within the first 3 years of monitoring.

ES&R monitoring data on initial densities will be important baseline information for tracking continued development of the plant community as it matures and for understanding initial densities that are necessary for successful control of invasive species. In the future, objectives that vary depending on the post-fire weather conditions may be a useful tool. These conditional objectives would be developed to include a range of values rather than a specific target objective. Eventually, given enough data on projects on similar ecological sites over time, a model could be developed to predict optimum seeding success over a range of conditions. Using such a dynamic approach for setting objectives would minimize the numbers of projects that are deemed failures due to setting of unrealistic objectives or due to environmental factors that are outside the control of land management.

Stratification

Each stratum (monitoring unit) within a treatment area must have a minimum of three plots to generate a mean and standard deviation. Therefore, each additional monitoring unit requires an increase in monitoring effort to establish these three plots. The time and effort required to monitor a post-fire project will often guide whether or not additional strata are included in the monitoring plan. We expect that different levels of stratification will occur at different projects and there is no way to standardize stratification. However, it is important to adequately describe properties of each monitoring unit (location, soils, topography, etc.) to define the scope of inference of collected data. Three useful rules to follow based on our experiences on the Vale burned areas are:

1. Base strata on the largest areas treated; do not spend time on areas that represent a small percentage of the treatment.

2. Try to measure at least five plots in each stratum.

3. Slopes that exceed 30% are difficult to perform the quantitative techniques on. Drill seedings typically do not exceed 20% slopes, but aerial seedings may exceed 30%. This means that monitoring aerial seedings in areas of greater than 30% slopes will require a different technique than that described here.

4. Previous land-management actions may be a more important factor in determining seeding success than edaphic or environmental factors. For example, the previous seeding at the Keeney Pass burned area affected success of the new seeding and should have been included as a stratification factor.

Random Sampling

Random sampling generally worked well. Plots assigned randomly occasionally occurred in locations that were not acceptable and had to be moved to another random location. Plots using the three-spoke design are fairly large, about 2.5 acres, and encompass considerable variation within them. This is a desirable factor when monitoring large areas such as post-fire rehabilitation treatments. However, sometimes portions of a plot can encompass areas that should not be sampled, or the shape of the landscape is such that it cannot accommodate the three-spoke design. In several cases, it was necessary to move the transects to violate the 120° degree separation between transects. This was primarily due to the transect intersecting an area that could not be drill seeded due to obstacles such as steep drainages or rock outcrops. When this occurs, care must be taken when moving transects. Transects should not be placed close enough together that double sampling of the belt transects occurs. Additionally, if these situations are expected to occur often, the plot design may need to be modified such as reducing the length or number of transects.

Control Plots

Control plots within project areas provide a direct measurement of treatment effects. This is important because control plots are often placed in adjacent, non-treated areas which may differ from areas proposed for treatment. This further increases the variability, thereby reducing our ability to detect changes due to the treatment. For drill seedings, it is simple to establish areas that are large enough to place an individual plot and then avoid seeding these areas. For aerial seedings, this is much more difficult. Control plots for aerial seedings can be placed in areas that are deliberately not seeded (although there may be some seed drift), or placed in areas that could have been seeded but were not due to logistical convenience (such as using roads as convenient boundaries).

In this monitoring effort, experience gained in the first and second year of monitoring allowed a determination of seeded versus non-seeded plants within treatment plots. In this case, an estimate of plant establishment could be made without the use of control plots; however, as plants grow larger and resemble pre-existing plants, it will become impossible to determine which were seeded and which were not. Therefore, control plots will be vital to determining long-term treatment effects at these post-fire rehabilitation projects.

Data Quality

To reduce variation in data, two actions can be taken: (1) improve stratification and (2) group species into functional groups rather than analyzing them separately. Improving stratification will result in lower variability and hence, lower estimated sample sizes. Those factors that most greatly influence the character of the pre-fire landscape should be considered for use as strata. This includes land-management activities such as recent seedings (and their success), grazing practices, and pre-fire vegetation. Knowledge of these pre-fire factors is essential for efficient stratification. Grouping species into functional groups often decreases standard deviations as compared to individual species standard deviations. In some cases, the majority of a functional group is composed of one species (for example, *A. cristatum* in the seeded grass functional group), and in these cases, individual species can be analyzed separately.

In some instances, it will not be possible to detect a difference between treatment and control plots due to high variability. Sample adequacy estimates for monitoring data at the Vale fires generally produced large required sample sizes for functional group cover or density. These sample size estimates are due to high natural variability in existing communities and in patchiness of seedling emergence and establishment of seeded species. As a result, variability around density and cover estimates may be high despite efforts to decrease variability through stratification. If, however, the difference between treatment and control (effect size) for a monitoring parameter is large, a confidence interval of the difference between treatment and control will likely not include zero, and a significant difference will be detected despite high variability.

Overall, one needs to determine what kind of a difference can be expected from a seeding. Does one expect a large difference that is apparent upon visual inspection of the area, or is it reasonable to expect a 5 or 10% difference in cover, density, or gap measurements as the result of seeding? Realistic expectations of data quality and variability need to be developed over time and used to develop reasonable objectives for future projects.

Summary statistics and confidence intervals of the difference were used for final comparisons of data at the treatment plots to the density objectives. This method was recommended in Wirth and Pyke (2007) as a way to display monitoring data variability as well as to provide a test of achieving objectives. Confidence intervals of the difference demonstrate not only the difference between treatment and control but uncertainty around these estimates, which, in many cases, is substantial. For this report, we provided confidence intervals of the difference for only quantitative density objectives because they are the most applicable in determining success of projects at these four fires. Constructing these graphs for other data, such as cover of functional groups or basal-gap intercept data, would show no difference between treatment and control in most instances because seeded plants are still immature at 3 years post-seeding. However, cover should increase annually depending on weather, albeit slowly, and basal gap may begin to decrease in the 3 years of ES&R-funded monitoring. These measures will be critical in determining the long-term effects of ES&R projects on pre-fire vegetation recover, seeded plant persistence, invasive species abundance, and site protection. Determining these long-term effects will require additional follow-up studies outside the 3-year time frame.

Performance of Quantitative Methods

Multiple issues arise during vegetation monitoring that can add variability to data. To enhance data quality and comparability, these issues should be addressed when they occur. While testing the monitoring strategy at burned areas in Oregon, we encountered issues associated with density data collection, species identification, initial differences between treatment and control plots, basal-gap intercept, and line-point intercept measurements. Below we describe issues we encountered with each of these techniques so that they can be recognized in early stages of future monitoring efforts.

Accurate collection of density data requires the objective identification of individual plants. This can be difficult when collecting data on seedlings, rhizomatous species, and residual grass plants. Therefore, strategies for dealing with these situations need to be developed and applied consistently to decrease variation among observers monitoring sample plots in different years.

Individual seedlings can be difficult to distinguish from emerging annual grasses, rhizomatous plants, or stray, non-reproductive tillers from existing bunchgrasses (fig. 19). For instance, drill seeding creates furrows (to a greater or lesser extent depending on the soil type and drill setting) that can separate existing bunchgrasses causing some tillers to appear separated from the mother plant. In the first year after a seeding, it is not necessary to identify seedlings to the species level, but it is important to accurately identify seeded grasses compared to existing grasses or annual grasses. Training observers about the characteristics of the target species seedlings is the first step. The second is calibrating the observations of multiple observers by collecting data from the same plots to ensure similarity of measurements. These steps can help alleviate errors generated due to identifying individual plants and having multiple field personnel in the same or different years.

Rhizomatous plants also can be difficult to quantify depending on how strongly rhizomatous they are. Strongly rhizomatous species can be relatively easily counted as tillers/ramets. Weakly rhizomatous species present difficulties. These species can be loose bunches or several tillers closely spaced with other tillers farther apart. Where individuals are difficult to distinguish, visually identifiable "bunches" should be counted. Bunches can be assumed to be individuals for all practical purposes, but the definition of individuals must be documented for each monitoring project. For strongly rhizomatous species, individual tillers are easily counted and should be the unit of interest. For seeded rhizomatous species, such as *Elymus lanceolatus* (thickspike wheatgrass), our experience is that in the first 3 years after a fire they tend to grow like bunchgrasses, presumably becoming more rhizomatous after they are well established.

Prior to collecting density data, observers should be familiar with growth forms and appearance of mature and seedling plants that grow in the area. Comparison to other plants outside plots can be made to determine differences between seedlings and non-seeded species. Control areas may assist in training observers on the appearances of existing plants in the area.

Figure 19. Photograph showing difficulty involved in identifying individuals within drill rows of new seedings.

Quadrat Sizes

It is necessary to use at least two different quadrat sizes to efficiently estimate density of all life forms at a plot. Typically, a belt transect that runs the entire length of a transect is adequate for large or adult plants of low to medium densities. Within this large quadrat, it is time consuming to count smaller or more abundant plants. These plants, along with seeded plants, can be counted using a smaller quadrat. For monitoring at the Vale burned areas, 10 1- x 1-m quadrats were placed along each transect, and densities of target plants were counted. This seemed to work well, but depending on the plant community, could also be adjusted to increase efficiency. Target plant species that did not have 10 individuals within the 30 1- x 1-m quadrats were counted in belt transects. Very small and abundant plants, such as *B. tectorum* were counted within subquadrats that were 0.2- x 0.2-m in size. This seemed to be a reasonable size as *B. tectorum* was very often abundant. Additionally, in a few instances, abundant rhizomatous grasses were also counted in these small subquadrats.

Size Classes

Size classes are useful for gauging relative age and size of grass species. Monitoring at the four Vale burned areas used three size classes. Size class A was an emerging seedling, B was a small, non-reproductive plant, and C was an established, reproductive adult. In practice, there are many plants that could be classified as a C one year and a B the next year. Tracking B and C size classes also takes time, particularly for rhizomatous plants. Therefore, these two size classes (B and C) have little use unless the percentage of plants reproducing in a given year needs to be determined. It is simpler and quicker to track seedlings and established plants using two size classes; however, some situations may call for using additional classes.

Species Identification

Some of the seeded species were difficult to distinguish between other seeded or non-seeded species without an inflorescence. Once inflorescences were present, it was possible to identify grasses to species, but not varietal level. The most problematic species to distinguish in the Vale burned areas were bluebunch wheatgrass (*P. spicata*) versus Snake River wheatgrass (*E. wawawaiensis*), as well as Siberian wheatgrass (*A. fragile*) versus crested or desert wheatgrass (*A. cristatum* or *A. desertorum*).

It was usually not possible to distinguish between *P. spicata* and *E. wawawaiensis* without reproductive structures. These two species were previously considered the same species. The difference was determined in the field by examining glumes, rachis, and leaves of each plant. The glumes of *E. wawawaiensis* are linear while the glumes of *P. spicata* are more obovate; however, there was much variation within this characteristic. In addition, *E. wawawaiensis* often showed a darker leaf color with the leaf blades slightly reflexed from the stem. This trait also was variable and more evident in older established plants. Another characteristic that was highly variable among the *P. spicata* plants was the length of the rachis, ranging from spikelets not overlapping to those with up to one-half their length overlapping. When the spikelets were overlapping, it was sometimes difficult to quickly distinguish between *P. spicata* and *E. lanceolatus*.

Agropyron fragile was seeded in areas with existing *A. cristatum* or *A. fragile* seedings. This made it difficult to determine small previously seeded plants from recently seeded plants. Additionally, morphological variation within these species often makes it difficult to quickly distinguish between them. The USDA PLANTS database (http://plants.usda.gov accessed 24 Mar 2009) distinguishes between *A. cristatum*, *A. desertorum*, and *A. fragile*, whereas Cronquist and others (1994) distinguished only *A. cristatum*, but provide a key to distinguish between *A. pectiniforme*, *A. cristatum*, and *A. fragile*. Cronquist and others (1994) combine *A. desertorum* with *A. fragile*. According to the USDA plant fact sheet on crested wheatgrass, *A. cristatum* ('fairway' crested wheatgrass) differs from *A. desertorum* ('standard' crested wheatgrass) in that it has shorter spikes and the spikes of *A. desertorum* can be comb-like to oblong whereas the spikes of *A. cristatum* are more widely spreading. During monitoring of these fires, plants with characteristics of both species were encountered, as well as plants that were intermediate between the two forms (possibly *A. cristatum* x *A. desertorum*). According to the USDA plant fact sheet, *A. fragile* is described as being very similar to *A. cristatum* and *A. desertorum* except that it has finer leaves, narrower and awnless glumes and lemmas and more ascending, sub-cylindrical spikelets. We encountered *A. fragile* plants that varied widely, including having short-awned glumes and slightly hairy spikelets.

The 'Sherman' cultivar of *P. secunda* also was commonly used in seedings in the area. This cultivar was easily distinguished from the native variety; however, species codes of the two were the same despite their vastly different sizes. According to the USDA PLANTS database *P. secunda* is a single species with a wide range in morphological variation whereas Cronquist and others (1994) recognize *P. ampla,* and some seed catalogs refer to it as *P. ampla* var. Sherman. Codes must be defined to distinguish between these two varieties in the monitoring data. USDA PLANTS database does retain unique synonyms for recognized former species and their use will aid in standardization and future comparisons. However, no codes exist for cultivars.

The problem of identification also extends to recently seeded plants that have not and will not flower in the year of monitoring. Although it may be possible to make an educated identification of species in these cases, it is time-consuming and less accurate than waiting until flowering. In these instances, it was better to classify the plant as "unknown seeded grass" and to wait until successive years for a positive identification.

Areas open to livestock grazing where inflorescences may be removed or absent, may create identification problems. In these cases, it may not be possible to identify to species even for adults. In these cases, a standard method of identifying species groups should be used. This can be done by recording the USDA plant symbols for the potential species in alphabetical order, separated by forward slashes. For example, in the situation where it is not possible to distinguish between crested wheatgrass and Siberian wheatgrass, the proper code would be AGCR/AGFR.

Initial Differences in Control and Treatment Plots

Initial differences in success indicators between control and treatment plots should be considered when analyzing and interpreting data. For example, if control plots have higher cover of pre-burn grasses than treatment plots, an increase in cover due to seeding will be more difficult to detect. This can be done by comparing changes between the first year to the third year for control and treatment plots rather than a direct comparison between plots in any given year.

Basal-Gap Intercept

Basal-gap intercept is a straightforward and generally repeatable procedure among years and observers. However, difficulties occur when there are large concentrations of amorphous grass clumps, as can happen in dense *P. secunda* stands (as seen at the Cow Hollow burn area) or in communities dominated by rhizomatous grasses. Additionally, in areas with dense, pre-fire plants, it is difficult to detect any changes in gaps resulting from the seeding, because seedlings are small and unlikely to stop basal gaps relative to mature, naturally recovering perennials. Observers are better able to detect changes using this technique when there are fewer pre-existing plants. In addition, this technique may be more useful for longer-term (5+ years post-seeding) monitoring of treatment and control plots since this length of time may be necessary for seeded plants to grow and begin to close gaps. A decision regarding the use of this procedure for the first 3 years monitoring should be made on a case-by-case basis.

The basal-gap intercept technique used on these fires included perennial forbs as stopping gaps. In retrospect, there is a large amount of variability in forb emergence and abundance from year-to-year and that probably introduces additional variation into basal-gap intercept data. Additionally, perennial exotic forbs also stop a gap (for example, *C. draba*). Invasive plants that can increase following a fire might be better ruled as non-stopping species for this technique. Without such a rule, basal-gap data may suggest an improvement in basal-gap intercept data when in fact the area is being invaded. If perennial forbs are included in gap measurements, it is necessary to document what species are stopping gaps.

Line-Point Intercept

Cover values for perennial grasses at the four fires generally showed changes from year one to three (some increases, some decreases) in both treatment and control plots. While these data were not separated into seeded and unseeded groupings, changes were primarily due to variations in the cover of pre-fire plants rather than seeded plants. Significant changes in cover due to seeded species, except in instances of a highly successful seeding, appear to occur after the 3-year time frame.

The line-point intercept procedure as described in Herrick and others (2005a) counts both live and standing dead herbaceous cover the same. After fire, where most herbaceous material is removed, cover will be the regenerating live material, and in the second year the regenerating live material plus the standing dead from the previous year. This may create an artifact of an increase in cover in the second year post-seeding as a result of the method. However, it does create an accurate view of the site protection from raindrop impact, a measure of protection from water erosion.

Cover is the best monitoring technique given the time expended in gathering the data for tracking the status of invasive annual plants. It allows a measurement of dominance of these species relative to the desired perennial plants. Gathering density data for these plants may be time-consuming because of the potentially high numbers of individuals (*e.g.*, > 10,000 plants/m^2, Mack and Pyke, 1983). Cover comparisons of invasive annual grasses between treatment and control plots will aid in determining if the seeding treatment alters the dominance of invasive plants.

Conclusions

There was a low level of plant establishment at all seedings from 2005. The primary reason for this level of establishment on all treatments except the Cow Hollow seeding was most likely the unfavorable timing and amount of precipitation in 2007 and 2008 (fig. 1). Excluding Cow Hollow, initial seeded perennial grass densities in 2006 ranged between 2.2 and 6.3 plants/m^2 while final densities ranged between 0.4 and 1.7 plants/m^2. There was an average mortality rate of 76% from 2006 to 2008 in these six treatments.

Target objectives for perennial grass density of future projects may wish to consider these results. To establish five plants/m^2 at the end of the 3-year monitoring period, density of emerging grasses would need to be much higher than those observed in the first spring after seeding. This level of plant emergence was not seen in 2006 despite adequate precipitation. Future projects might consider either increasing their seeding rates on these sites (Pyke and Archer, 1991) or lowering target density objectives in these areas. Additionally, the general state of pre-fire vegetation should be considered when developing these target objectives. For instance, the Double Mountain non-native seeding was primarily composed of exotic annuals prior to the fire. The seeding in this area resulted in less seedling establishment than the Double Mountain native seeding where the pre-fire vegetation was composed of less cover of exotic annuals and more cover of native perennials.

The maximum density objective of 100 *B. tectorum* plants/m^2 was likewise not met and may not be achievable under any circumstances. *Bromus tectorum* densities were 4 to 12 times higher than the objective. Based on our observations, *B. tectorum* densities may have increased after drill seeding due to soil disturbance, followed by a gradual decrease over time. At the same time, *B. tectorum* density is highly correlated with environmental factors such as precipitation and rodent activity, which may override site differences (Mack and Pyke, 1983). Due to this variation and the small size of seeded plants, a reasonable target for *B. tectorum* density is difficult to determine within the first 3 years. Such a realistic objective for *B. tectorum* density would need to vary depending on the postfire weather conditions and the amount of disturbance due to treatment application. Objectives related to *B. tectorum* cover on seeded versus control plots might be an alternative objective to consider. An example target objective might be to maintain or decrease *B. tectorum* cover on seeded areas relative to controls.

Measurements of density within the first 3 years provide the best estimate of initial seeding success. Increases in cover due to seedings were not detectable in the first 3 years following seeding in this monitoring effort. Changes in cover resulting from treatments may be detectable in cases where seedings are highly successful in the first 3 years following seeding, but based on observations from experience from the Vale burned area, this may require several consecutive years of above average precipitation to occur.

Although cover of seeded species may not be a good indication of seeding success in early years after treatment, it is useful for monitoring initial patterns of abundance of naturally recovering vegetation, exotic annual grasses and forbs, and bare ground. Cover of perennial grasses that survived the fire were substantial in some areas. In some cases, this was due primarily to shallow-rooted, perennial grasses (*P. secunda*) while in other areas, natural recovery consisted of both deep and shallow-rooted perennial grasses. Identifying the level of natural recovery at a treatment area establishes a baseline for long-term assessments of treatment effects. Cover measurements at these four fires also revealed patterns common to most of the treatment areas in cover of litter, bare ground, and exotic annuals in response to drill seeding and weather patterns.

There was a rapid increase in litter at all treatments after fires. In 2006, there was an average of 43.5 and 25.7% litter cover in the control and treatment plots, respectively. By 2008, litter cover had increased to 73.6% in the control plots and 70.4% in the treatment plots. Overall, there was less litter in treatment than in control plots in 2006, probably due to the mechanical action of the seed drill. The exception to this trend was the Double Mountain non-native control plots, which had nearly as much litter cover in 2006 as in 2008. The Double Mountain non-native treatment plots had lower litter cover in 2006 than the control plots, further supporting the idea that the seed drill reduces litter cover in the initial years after treatment. Based on data from this monitoring, it appears that the reduction of litter cover due to drill seeding only lasts 2 to 3 years. Litter found in the control and treatment plots, albeit much of it from *B. tectorum*, acts to protect the soil surface from raindrop impact and subsequent erosion.

54

Not surprisingly, there was a corresponding decrease in bare ground from 2006 to 2008. At control plots, bare ground decreased from 17.2 to 9.3%, whereas bare ground at treatment plots decreased from 24.3 to 12.0%. Initially, higher percentages of bare ground at treatment plots appear to be due to the mechanical action of the drill. Two treatments, the Keeney Pass and Double Mountain non-native seedings, did not follow this trend. At these treatments, bare ground percentages in the control stayed nearly the same in 2006 and 2007. In these areas, the fire may not have been intense enough to reduce the litter on the ground and expose bare soil.

Cover of annual grasses, primarily *B. tectorum*, increased from 2006 to 2007 and then decreased slightly in 2008. This pattern was observed in all treatments except the Double Mountain native seeding treatment. In 2006, *B. tectorum* plants were large, probably due to the postfire nutrient flush and above average precipitation. In 2007, density and cover increased due to the high seed production in 2006. In 2008, plants were small due to low precipitation, but abundant from the large cohort of the previous year. Density in 2008 was generally similar to 2007 with some treatments increasing and decreasing slightly or remaining at the same levels. In general, the first year after fire resulted in lower densities of *B. tectorum* due to the loss of seed from the fire but very robust plants. Highest cover and density of exotic annual grasses occurred in the second year following fire due to the first year nutrient flush. However, the pattern observed at the Vale fire burned areas may change depending on different precipitation regimes and site factors.

At treatment areas, there was a consistent, negative linear relationship between the amount of cover of existing perennial grasses and annual grass cover. This relationship was also apparent in the gap data where annual grass cover was greatest when basal gaps in the >200 cm size class were more frequent. These relationships indicate the inverse nature of the relationship between presence of perennial grasses and annual grass cover, and this suggests that ES&R seedings, when successful, may improve rangeland status where annual invasive grasses are problematic.

There was generally low plant mortality throughout the four burned areas that were monitored (personal observation). All four fires burned in late July and early August. The last significant rainfall prior to the fires was the mid-May 2005. This rainfall may not have been adequate to keep perennial plants active, resulting in dormancy by the time of the fire. Future monitoring of plant mortality combined with fire timing and weather immediately prior to the disturbance may provide some capacity to predict when severe mortality will occur, thus aiding decisions on when post-fire rehabilitation seedings are necessary. Additional techniques for determining when and where natural recovery will occur are also needed to maximize treatment efficiency.

Overall, quantitative objectives are a valuable part of monitoring the initial success of post-fire seedings; however, they need to be adapted for specific sites and adjusted when required. The potential of a particular area to reach a certain level of density or cover of desirable plant species (for example, ecological site descriptions) and the condition of the pre-fire plant community (for example, healthy or degraded) can be used to set initial objectives, which could be further modified by conditional statements that depend on environmental conditions after seeding. These conditional objectives may be developed to include a range of values rather than a specific target objective. Eventually, given enough data from many projects over time, a model could be developed to predict optimum seeding success over a range of conditions. Using such a dynamic approach to setting objectives would minimize the numbers of projects that are deemed failures due to unrealistic objectives or environmental factors that are outside the control of land management.

Monitoring at the four 2005 burned areas from the Vale, Oregon district of the BLM demonstrated the potential uses and difficulties associated with monitoring ES&R treatment effectiveness. Overall, the monitoring approach combined with the quantitative techniques performed reasonably well in burned areas previously dominated by sagebrush. Problems encountered using the method were primarily logistical (for example, time required, stratification, or density-data collection) or due to the high variability of the natural communities.

Future monitoring efforts should take into account logistical constraints of each design element and quantitative technique to arrive at the most cost-effective yet statistically valid monitoring plan. In the future, procedures that encompass more of the natural variability either through less intense field methods at more locations or the use of remote sensing may be able to capture more of the natural variability at the landscape scale.

The value of the three quantitative techniques for interpreting success of post-fire seedings depends upon the time frame in which they will be used. For the first 3 years following seeding (the period for which monitoring is usually funded), density is the most directly applicable measurement of treatment effect and is emphasized in this report. Changes in plant cover and basal-gap intercept measurements are small during the first 3 years and, when combined with environmental and observer variation, could not be used for determining success. As the seeding ages and plants become larger, however, comparison of cover and gap-intercept data between treatment and control plots can be used to determine long-term effects. Further investigation is needed to determine whether initial densities in the first 3 years correlate to later cover and basal-gap intercept measurements.

In addition to assessing the level of establishment at a variety of different postfire seedings, using similar techniques to monitor several treatment areas enabled identification of common patterns. Consistent patterns of vegetation attributes identified in these four fires include the rate of accumulation of litter and decrease in bare ground cover, the inverse relationship between annual grass and forb cover, and the relationships between annual grasses, perennial grass cover and basal gap. Identifying additional patterns at a greater number of projects in a wider geographic area and correlating with site factors (such as soil, elevation, and climate) will aid efforts to improve seeding success through adaptive management.

Acknowledgments

The Bureau of Land Management provided primary funding for this project (USGS - BLM Interagency Agreement #HAI040045). We would specifically like to thank Jack Hamby (BLM, WO) and David Repass (BLM, WO) and the ES&R Monitoring Advisory Board: Jan Beyers (USFS, PSWRS), Robert Burton (BLM, NV), Jack Brown (BLM, UT), Sharon Paris (BLM, ID), Mike Pellant (BLM, ID), Pete Robichaud (USFS, RMRS), Mitch Thomas (BLM, OR), John Willoughby (BLM, CA) and Brian Watts (BLM, OR).

We also would like to thank USGS staff that have helped with field work, offered advice, and helped with report preparation: Kevin Knutson, Meagan Gates, Kimberly Klein, Malinda Choitz, Andrew Lindgren, Nicole DeCrappeo, Scott Shaff, Susan Powell, Janet Erickson, Ruth Jacobs, Nichole Roberts, Kate Kitchell, and Sue Phillips.

References Cited

Bureau of Land Management, 2005a, Keeney Pass fire (B3LE) emergency stabilization plan: Vale District, Malheur Resource Area, Oregon State Office, 19 p.

Bureau of Land Management, 2005b, Double Mountain fire (B2EY) emergency stabilization plan: Vale District, Malheur Resource Area, Oregon State Office, 20 p.

Bureau of Land Management, 2005c, Farewell Bend fire (B2AK) emergency stabilization plan: Vale District, Baker Resource Area, Oregon State Office, 16 p.

Bureau of Reclamation *http://www.usbr.gov/pn/agrimet/yearrpt.html* for station ONTO. Last accessed November 20, 2008.

Cronquist A., Holmgren, A.H., Holmgren, N.H., Reveal, J.L., and Holmgren, P.K., 1977, Intermountain flora: Vascular plants of the Intermountain West, USA, v. 6: The Monocotyledons, New York, Columbia University Press, 584 p.

Di Stefano, J., 2004, A confidence interval approach to data analysis: Forest Ecology and Management, v. 187, p. 173-183.

Elzinga, C.L., Salzer, D.W., and Willoughby, J.W., 1998, Measuring and monitoring plant populations: USDI BLM Technical Reference 1730-1, National Business Center, Denver, CO, 492 p.

Herrick, J.E., Van Zee, J.W., Havstad, K.M., Burkett, L.M., Whitford, W.G., 2005a, Monitoring manual for grassland, shrubland, and savanna ecosystems, v. 1, Quick Start: USDA-ARS Jornada Experimental Range, Las Cruces, NM, 36 p.

Herrick, J.E., Van Zee, J.W., Havstad, K.M., Burkett, L.M., Whitford, W.G., 2005b, Monitoring manual for grassland, shrubland, and savanna ecosystems, v. 2: Design, supplementary methods and interpretation: USDA-ARS Jornada Experimental Range, Las Cruces, NM, 200 p.

Mack, R.N., and Pyke, D.A., 1983, The demography of *Bromus Tectorum*: Variation in time and space: Journal of Ecology, v. 71, p. 69-93.

Natural Resource Conservation Service, 1997, Soil survey of the Baker County area, Oregon:

Oregon Climate Service, 2008, PRISM Group, Oregon State University, http://prism.oregonstate.edu/ accessed November 27, 2008.

Oregon State University Agricultural Experiment Station, USDA Soil Conservation Service, and Oregon Water Resources Board, 1969, Oregon's long-range requirements for water: General Soil Map Report with Irrigable Areas Malheur River Drainage Basin, Appendix I-10: Burns, Oregon, 85 p.

Pyke, D.A., and Archer, S., 1991, Plant-plant interactions affecting plant establishment and persistence on revegetated rangeland: Journal of Range Management, v. 44, p. 550-557.

Society for Range Management, 1999, A glossary of terms used in range management: Society for Range Management, Denver, Colorado, 20 p.

Wirth, T.A., and Pyke, D.A., 2007, Monitoring post-fire vegetation rehabilitation projects - A common approach for non-forested ecosystems: U.S. Geological Survey Scientific Investigations Report 2006-5048, 36 p.

Vallentine, J.F., 1971, Range development and improvements: Brigham Young University Press, Provo, Utah.

Appendix A. Monitoring Plot Locations and Soils

Table A1. Locations, slope, aspect, primary and secondary landscape types for monitoring plots at the four fires monitored.

[Note: Soil information for (Oregon Water Resources Board 1969) for all fires except Farewell Bend which is from the Baker county soil survey. Soil column is the mapping unit that the plot sits on according to the soil survey. Texture column is texture from sampling at each plot]

Plot name	Northing	Easting	Elevation (ft)	Elevation (m)	Slope	Aspect	Landscape type	Secondary
CH-NS-C01	4856367	487463	2,673	815	5	105	Hills/Mountains	Shoulder
CH-NS-C02	4855414	486268	2,739	835	11	112	Hills/Mountains	Backslope
CH-NS-C03	4856192	486675	2,729	832	5	348	Hills/Mountains	Toeslope
CH-NS-C04	4855468	486876	2,755	840	5	193	Hills/Mountains	Backslope
CH-NS-T02	4856581	487082	2,690	820	4	18	Hills/Mountains	Footslope
CH-NS-T03	4855175	486190	2,690	820	6	194	Hills/Mountains	Footslope
CH-NS-T04	4855124	487235	2,772	845	4	80	Hills/Mountains	Shoulder
CH-NS-T05	4854743	487200	2,673	815	7	315	Hills/Mountains	Backslope
CH-NS-T06	4856537	486532	2,723	830	2	356	Hills/Mountains	Shoulder
DM-NN-C00	4860202	467371	2,690	820	10	90	Hills/Mountains	Shoulder
DM-NN-C02	4860424	466523	2,960	902	2	66	Basin	na
DM-NN-C03	4859302	467516	2,624	800	5	46	Hills/Mountains	Shoulder
DM-NN-T02	4859511	467619	2,608	795	2	58	Hills/Mountains	Summit
DM-NN-T03	4860303	467983	2,575	785	2	45	Basin	na
DM-NN-T05	4859756	466362	2,723	830	2	346	Basin	na
DM-NS-C01	4854569	476782	2,903	885	2	42	Hills/Mountains	Shoulder
DM-NS-C05	4853774	475215	2,772	845	4	350	Hills/Mountains	Summit
DM-NS-C06	4851989	473090	3,133	955	6	2	Hills/Mountains	Toeslope
DM-NS-C07	4849813	475005	3,362	1025	9	348	Hills/Mountains	Footslope
DM-NS-T07	4855491	474739	2,608	795	3	104	Basin	na
DM-NS-T08	4854627	477005	2,854	870	12	99	Hills/Mountains	Shoulder
DM-NS-T10	4852314	473629	3,133	955	4	0	Hills/Mountains	Toeslope
DM-NS-T11	4850563	474072	3,402	1037	5	78	Hills/Mountains	Backslope
DM-NS-T14	4850586	474992	3,264	995	10	64	Hills/Mountains	Backslope
DM-NS-T15	4851221	475377	3,133	955	11	56	Hills/Mountains	Shoulder
DM-NS-T17	4849503	476094	3,248	990	6	298	Hills/Mountains	Backslope

ID								
FB-NN-C01	4909064	476536	2,690	820	5	161	Hills/Mountains	Footslope
FB-NN-C05	4908227	476077	2,690	820	10	64	Hills/Mountains	Backslope
FB-NN-C06	4909215	475864	2,706	825	12	179	Hills/Mountains	Footslope
FB-NN-T01	4908379	476163	2,657	810	8	80	Hills/Mountains	Toeslope
FB-NN-T02	4908658	475932	2,706	825	14	166	Hills/Mountains	Backslope
FB-NN-T03	4908087	475580	2,739	835	7	130	Hills/Mountains	Summit
FB-NS-C02	4906745	474857	3,018	920	14	43	Hills/Mountains	Shoulder
FB-NS-C03	4906808	473022	3,215	980	3	169	Basin	na
FB-NS-C04	4907656	474972	2,854	870	12	158	Hills/Mountains	Footslope
FB-NS-T06	4907367	475087	2,788	850	14	104	Hills/Mountains	Footslope
FB-NS-T07	4906637	473895	3,083	940	14	206	Hills/Mountains	Toeslope
FB-NS-T08	4908076	475100	2,887	880	18	90	Hills/Mountains	Backslope
KP-NN-C05	4859314	488118	2,680	817	6	222	Hills/Mountains	Footslope
KP-NN-C06	4858804	488477	2,624	800	7	215	Hills/Mountains	Toeslope
KP-NN-C07	4858777	487938	2,673	815	5	73	Hills/Mountains	Backslope
KP-NN-T06	4858765	488209	2,624	800	5	93	Hills/Mountains	Backslope
KP-NN-T07	4857179	489686	2,793	851	4	215	Hills/Mountains	Other
KP-NN-T08	4858537	488852	2,624	800	6	175	Hills/Mountains	Footslope
KP-NS-C01	4861095	489184	2,739	835	8	6	Hills/Mountains	Footslope
KP-NS-C02	4858072	489652	2,690	820	13	48	Hills/Mountains	Backslope
KP-NS-C03	4857311	490616	2,608	795	10	44	Hills/Mountains	Backslope
KP-NS-C04	4860146	489444	2,762	842	7	175	Hills/Mountains	Footslope
KP-NS-C08	4860191	487171	2,700	823	9	240	Hills/Mountains	Toeslope
KP-NS-T02	4859438	490249	2,673	815	4	112	Flat Plain	na
KP-NS-T03	4860784	488830	2,788	850	11	348	Hills/Mountains	Backslope
KP-NS-T04	4860735	488139	2,903	885	6	87	Hills/Mountains	Backslope
KP-NS-T05	4859436	487718	2,706	825	10	77	Hills/Mountains	Backslope

Table A2. Soil classification units, series, and measured surface textures at each monitoring plot.

[Ny = Nyssa Silt Loam (tentative series from Oregon Water Resources Board, 1969). Ma = unnamed Silt Loam (tentative series from Oregon Water Resources Board, 1969). Unit 60 = Moderately fine-textured, well drained soils on gently sloping hills underlain by lakebed sediments. Typically a loamy surface (0-7") and a clay loam subsurface (7-24"). Unit 75 = Loamy, shallow well drained soils over bedrock of basalt, rhyolite, or tuff. Typically a stoney silt loam (0-5") underlain by a loam subsurface layer (5-12"). Unit 79 = Loamy, deep, well-drained soils developed from wind deposits. Typically loam to silt loam throughout (0-48"). Unit 94 = Raw sediments (small acreages). Unit 98 = Steep raw sediments (small acreages). 122C = Poall very fine sandy loam (very fine sandy loam underlain by clay). 143 = Ruckles-Rucklick Complex (Ruckles = very stoney clay loam underlain by clay - very cobbly silt loam underlain by silty clay loam) 124D = Poall very fine sandy loam (very fine sandy loam underlain by clay)]

Plot name	Soil	Soil series	Actual surface texture 0-5 cm
CH-NS-C01	Ny	Nyssa Silt Loam	Silt Loam
CH-NS-C02	Ny 94	Nyssa Silt Loam - Raw Sediments	Silt Loam
CH-NS-C03	Ny	Nyssa Silt Loam	Silt Loam
CH-NS-C04	Ny 94	Nyssa Silt Loam - Raw Sediments	Silt Loam
CH-NS-T02	Ny	Nyssa Silt Loam	Silt Loam
CH-NS-T03	Ny 94	Nyssa Silt Loam - Raw Sediments	Silt Loam
CH-NS-T04	Ny 94	Nyssa Silt Loam - Raw Sediments	Silt Loam
CH-NS-T05	Ny 94	Nyssa Silt Loam - Raw Sediments	Silt Loam
CH-NS-T06	Ny	Nyssa Silt Loam	Silt Loam
DM-NN-C00	60-79-94	Unit 60 - Unit 79 - Raw Sediments	Sandy Loam
DM-NN-C02	60-79-94	Unit 60 - Unit 79 - Raw Sediments	Sandy Loam
DM-NN-C03	60-79-94	Unit 60 - Unit 79 - Raw Sediments	Sandy Loam
DM-NN-T02	60-79-94	Unit 60 - Unit 79 - Raw Sediments	Sandy Loam
DM-NN-T03	60-79-94	Unit 60 - Unit 79 - Raw Sediments	Sandy Loam
DM-NN-T05	60-79-98	Unit 60 - Unit 79 - Steep Raw Sediments	Sandy Loam
DM-NS-C01	Ny 94	Nyssa Silt Loam - Raw Sediments	Loamy Sand
DM-NS-C05	Ny 94	Nyssa Silt Loam - Raw Sediments	Silty Loam
DM-NS-C06	75-60	Unit 75 - Unit 60	Sandy Clay Loam
DM-NS-C07	75	Unit 75	Loam
DM-NS-T07	Ny 94	Nyssa Silt Loam - Raw Sediments	Sandy Loam
DM-NS-T08	Ny 94	Nyssa Silt Loam - Raw Sediments	Loamy Sand
DM-NS-T10	75-60	Unit 75 - Unit 60	Sandy Loam
DM-NS-T11	75	Unit 75	Loam

61

		Unit 75	
DM-NS-T14	75		Loam/Sandy Loam
DM-NS-T15	Ny 94	Nyssa Silt Loam - Raw Sediments	Loam
DM-NS-T17	Ny 94	Nyssa Silt Loam - Raw Sediments	Loam
FB-NN-C01	143	Ruckles-Rucklick Complex	Silty Clay
FB-NN-C05	143	Ruckles-Rucklick Complex	Clay Loam
FB-NN-C06	143	Ruckles-Rucklick Complex	Clay Loam
FB-NN-T01	124D/143	Poall Very Fine Sandy Loam / Ruckles-Rucklick Complex	Clay Loam
FB-NN-T02	124D/143	Poall Very Fine Sandy Loam / Ruckles-Rucklick Complex	Clay
FB-NN-T03	143	Ruckles-Rucklick Complex	Silty Clay Loam
FB-NS-C02	143	Ruckles-Rucklick Complex	Silty Clay Loam
FB-NS-C03	143	Ruckles-Rucklick Complex	Clay
FB-NS-C04	143	Ruckles-Rucklick Complex	Clay loam/Clay
FB-NS-T06	124D/143	Poall Very Fine Sandy Loam / Ruckles-Rucklick Complex	Clay Loam
FB-NS-T07	122C/143	Poall Very Fine Sandy Loam / Ruckles-Rucklick Complex	Clay
FB-NS-T08	143	Ruckles-Rucklick Complex	Sandy Clay
KP-NN-C05	Ny 94	Nyssa Silt Loam - Raw Sediments	Silt Loam
KP-NN-C06	Ny 94	Nyssa Silt Loam - Raw Sediments	Silt Loam
KP-NN-C07	Ny 94	Nyssa Silt Loam - Raw Sediments	Silt Loam
KP-NN-T06	Ny 94	Nyssa Silt Loam - Raw Sediments	Silt Loam
KP-NN-T07	Ny 94	Nyssa Silt Loam - Raw Sediments	Silt Loam
KP-NN-T08	Ny 94	Nyssa Silt Loam - Raw Sediments	Silt Loam
KP-NS-C01	Ny Ma	Nyssa Silt Loam - Unnamed Silt Loam	Silt Loam
KP-NS-C02	Ny Ma	Nyssa Silt Loam - Unnamed Silt Loam	Silt Loam
KP-NS-C03	Ny Ma / Ny 94	Nyssa Silt Loam - Unnamed Silt Loam/ Nyssa Silt Loam - Raw Sediments	Silt Loam
KP-NS-C04	Ny Ma	Nyssa Silt Loam - Unnamed Silt Loam	Silt Loam
KP-NS-C08	Ny	Nyssa Silt Loam	Silt Loam
KP-NS-T02	Ny Ma	Nyssa Silt Loam - Unnamed Silt Loam	Silt Loam
KP-NS-T03	Ny Ma	Nyssa Silt Loam - Unnamed Silt Loam	Silt Loam
KP-NS-T04	Ny Ma	Nyssa Silt Loam - Unnamed Silt Loam	Silt Loam
KP-NS-T05	Ny 94	Nyssa Silt Loam - Raw Sediments	Silt Loam

www.ingramcontent.com/pod-product-compliance
Lightning Source LLC
Chambersburg PA
CBHW080436290526
45791CB00008BA/2519